Muzzleloading Essentials

Hunting Wisdom Library™

NORTH★AMERICAN★HUNTING★CLUB

MINNETONKA, MINNESOTA

About the Author

Bryce M. Towsley is an award-winning writer and photographer whose work covers a wide diversity of subjects, but none more than the field of big game hunting and the firearms used for that sport.

In the past two decades, Towsley has published hundreds of articles and thousands of photos in many of the major outdoor and gun magazines. This is his third hunting-related book and his second for NAHC.

Towsley is an admitted gun buff and has been shooting muzzleloaders for more than three decades. He is an avid hunter with more than 35 years of experience, taking his first whitetail in Vermont in 1966 at the age of eleven. Since then, he has hunted extensively throughout the United States and Canada as well as in Mexico, Africa and Europe for a wide variety of game.

This is for Erin and Nathan, my best hunting buddies. – B.T.

MUZZLELOADING ESSENTIALS

Tom Carpenter
Director of Book Development

Heather Koshiol
Sr. Book Development Coordinator

Jenya Prosmitsky
Art Director

Shari Gross
Production Designer

Phil Aarrestad
Commissioned Photography

Dan Kennedy
Photo Editor

Special thanks to:
Traditions Performance Firearms
Thompson/Center Arms

PHOTO CREDITS

All photos by Bryce Towsley except: Charles Alsheimer 65 (bottom), 76, 98, 122, 132, 136, 147; **Chuck Carpenter** 78, 121 (both); **Gary Clancy** 8, 29 (top), 35, 40, 41, 43 (both bottom), 52 (bottom), 61, 71 (bottom), 80, 138, 146; **Donald Jones** 51 (bottom), 91 (top), 93 (top), 94 (top), 95 (bottom), 142 (bottom); **Mark Kayser** 56 (bottom), 86 (both), 112 (top), 128 (left), 151; **Lee Kline** 36 (bottom), 92 (top); **Knight Muzzleloaders** 16 (bottom left); **Bill Marchel** 12 (bottom), 67, 89 (top), 134 (bottom); NAHC cover onlay, 95 (top); **NAHC/Billy Linder Photography** 1, 100, 108, 110, 116, 117 (right center), 139; **NAHC/Tom Carpenter** 37, 102 (top), 114 (bottom); **Justin Robinson** 87; **Jim Shockey** 32, 39 (bottom), 89 (bottom), 93 (bottom); **Ron Spomer** 54; **T/C Arms** 77 (right), 117 (top right), 118 (top left, left center, bottom left, top right, right center bottom), 120 (bottom left, top right). Illustrations on pages 11, 12, 18 by **Dave Schelitzche**.

2 3 4 5 6 7 8 / 04 03 02

ISBN 1-58159-138-1

North American Hunting Club
12301 Whitewater Drive
Minnetonka, Minnesota 55343
www.huntingclub.com

Table of Contents

Foreword

I wish this book had been in my hands when I was planning my first muzzleloader hunt.

As I stood by my mailbox looking at a muzzleloaders-only Wyoming pronghorn license, I broke a little sweat and it wasn't from the midsummer heat. Now I had to make good on my commitment to get familiar and proficient with a muzzleloader before September.

Oh, the trials and tribulations. Started out with a sidelock. Tried many loads. Fretted about bullet choices. Stuck a peep sight on and sighted-in. Attempted to clean the thing. How should I swab out between shots? Got patches stuck, but *good*. Endured horrible hangfires.

But I learned, learned to like the sidelock, got fairly efficient with it, but moved on to an in-line muzzleloader. A whole new learning process evolved, but finally I was ready to hunt.

Through it all, the author of this book, Bryce Towsley, answered many of my questions. I bugged him night and day. It's a miracle he ever finished writing. I was lucky he was there. You're lucky too—because he has put forth his vast muzzleloading knowledge right here, in *Muzzleloading Essentials*, exclusively for North American Hunting Club members.

This is a bible on muzzleloaders—the mystique, the details—from flintlocks to sidelocks to modern in-lines. You'll learn how to properly load, sight in, shoot, clean, maintain, improve performance, hunt successfully. Hundreds of tips fill these pages as well!

These truly are the essentials of muzzleloading, brought to you by an author who, quite simply, shoots a lot of critters each year with guns loaded from the front.

The Wyoming hunt? A learning experience. Stalked a good antelope. Plumb missed. Made another stalk the next day: misfire—trigger assembly was greased too generously and gun wouldn't go off. Antelope laughed.

Finally I crawled a half-mile in the wheel-ruts of a circle-field irrigator to within 50 yards of a good doe, said a little prayer, squeezed the trigger, and two Pyrodex pellets sent a bullet on its way from 50 yards. I did it!

Muzzleloader hunting is here to stay. Whether you're starting out too, or are a frontloader veteran, *Muzzleloading Essentials* will help you too find success more often.

Tom

Tom Carpenter
Editor—North American Hunting Club Books

INTRODUCTION

For more than 200 years, firearms hunters used muzzle-loading rifles for one simple reason: They had to. Today, hunters use muzzleloaders because they want to, and therein lies a world of difference.

To think that the mountain men of the 19th century would have chosen front-stuffing, blackpowder, single-shot rifles to battle grizzly bears if they had the option of repeating, bolt-action .338 Magnums is foolish. Those guys didn't care about the "romance" of a muzzleloader; they wanted to stay alive and would always pick the best tool available to them. At the time, the best tool was a muzzleloader.

But if we could somehow take a repeating rifle back in time with us, you can bet there would be a beaver pelt bidding war the likes of which will never be seen on eBay.

If a hunter is using a muzzleloader today, it's because he has elected to deliberately make hunting more difficult. This idea of making the sport "challenging" is a very new and modern concept.

Unlike our ancestors, we no longer hunt for our survival. We hunt because we enjoy it and we hunt because we are compelled by our genetic code to hunt. Game laws and modern realities limit our time spent hunting and the number of animals we can shoot, so modern hunters have decided to make hunting more challenging. One way we do that is by limiting the tools with which we hunt: Mountain men would find that appalling, but modern hunters find it appealing.

That leads us to the modern muzzleloader hunter. It's a choice. One that makes hunting more interesting, more challenging and more satisfying. It connects us with our past—when hunting meant survival. And it brings us to the present—where hunting fills more personal needs that cannot and must not be measured at the game pole.

Bryce

—Bryce Towsley

Chapter 1

MUZZLELOADING RIFLES

*I*ndividualism is what makes this country great, and few segments of society are more segmented by individualism than the bunch we call hunters. If we all thought the same way, only one muzzleloader would exist. But what you like probably isn't what I like; the great thing is that we get to choose.

The traditionalist probably likes a flintlock shooting a round ball patched with pillow ticking and lubricated with bear grease. His muzzleloader most certainly propels the bullet with pure blackpowder. And perhaps he even made the bullet or the powder in his garage. He probably wears buckskin clothes and carries a knife that was hand-forged over an open fire. The sights on his gun are simple, open style, and he is as happy as a pig rolling in mud when he hunts this way. If he were forced to use a "modern" muzzleloader, he might think he had journeyed to his final reward and somehow things had been tragically mixed up.

The modern hunter is probably shooting a stainless steel, in-line muzzleloader with a synthetic stock. Ignition is with a #209 shotgun primer that lights a couple of Pyrodex Pellets. His solid-copper, hollow-point bullet is cased in a sabot of high-tech polymer and his gun is aimed with a 3-9X scope. He is protected from the rain by a Gore-Tex suit, and if you made him switch to "traditional" equipment he would stay home and watch reruns on television.

Variety is much more than merely the spice of life; it is life's very essence. And on the subject of muzzleloader hunting rifles, variety is more than a buzzword. It's a definition of what's available.

FLINTLOCK RIFLES

The first muzzleloader guns required that the shooter carry a burning "punk" around with him. When he was ready to shoot, he would pour some powder in a pan and stick the "match" in it to fire the gun. (Talk about long lock times!)

Obviously, this system had some flaws, not the least of which was that to do it correctly, the shooter needed at least three hands.

The next technological advance came in about 1411 A.D. The "matchlock" was conceived when some smart fellow got the idea of clamping the burning "match" in a mechanism that was tripped by a trigger and dropped into the priming pan to ignite the powder. It was burdensome to keep the match burning all the time, and there were many other problems, but the matchlock represented a big improvement over holding the match in your hand while trying to fire the gun.

The wheel-lock came next. The working wheel-lock is credited to Kehfuss of Nuremberg in about 1517. It used a serrated wheel that was wound against a spring. Pulling the trigger released the wheel to spin against a piece of flint, throwing off a shower of sparks and lighting the priming powder. It was sort of a prototype of the first Zippo cigarette lighter.

Next came the Snaphaunce, named for snaaphans, who were poultry thieves. The glowing "match" of a matchlock showed in the dark and gave away thieves' positions during their night-time raids, leading to beheadings and other unfortunate events. The snaaphans ironically complained that wheel-lock guns were too expensive. If they couldn't afford the "good guns" then perhaps they should have tried stealing something more valuable than chickens. So instead, the

Flintlock rifles were in use from the early 1600s until well into the percussion era. Today's hunter will find an additional challenge in using a flintlock.

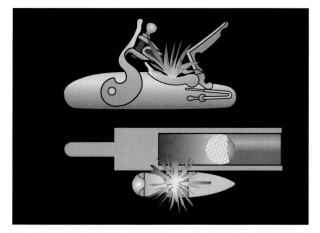

The flint strikes the frizzen (top), sending a shower of sparks into the priming pan and producing a flash from the priming powder (bottom) that ignites the powder in the barrel.

is hinged at the rear, and as the flint strikes, it pushes the frizzen back, pivoting the cover open to expose the priming powder.

At the same time, the flint scrapes along the face of the frizzen, throwing off a shower of sparks with the expectation that some will land in the priming powder and ignite it. The priming powder then burns through the "touch hole," which is a small hole drilled in the rear of the barrel that provides a path from the priming pan to the powder charge in the barrel. The sparks light a fire in the charge and send the bullet on its way.

It all works surprisingly well if the shooter knows what he is doing. In fact, it worked so well that many explorers and Native Americans continued to use flintlocks well into the era of percussion rifles. The shooters knew they could always find flint in the wilderness, but percussion caps, which must be manufactured, were often hard to locate.

The flint strikes the frizzen and sends a shower of sparks into the priming pan.

thieves came up with an early, crude flintlock.

Experts can't agree just when this crude flintlock evolved, but most think it was between 1525 and 1570. The gun used a piece of pyrites or flint held between jaws on the end of a spring-tensioned cock. It released when the trigger was pulled and struck a glancing blow against a steel anvil, sending a shower of sparks into the priming powder.

THE "MODERN" FLINTLOCK

About 1615, Marin le Bourgeoys of France invented the flintlock as we know it, and it hung around until well into the percussion era. The flintlock is a hammer that holds a piece of flint in a set of vice-like jaws. The flint is napped to a sharp edge in the front, and when the trigger is pulled, the hammer swings forward with the sharp edge leading. The flint strikes a "frizzen," which is a metal faceplate attached to a cover over the pan that holds the priming powder. The cover/frizzen

The vast majority of today's modern muzzleloader hunters elect to use guns ignited by percussion caps or by other types of impact-sensitive primers and, other than with hard-core traditionalists, the flintlock sees only limited use. But hunters who have tried it know that hunting big game with a flintlock is much more challenging and provides a tighter connection with muzzleloading's roots. In my rarely humble opinion, every hunter should try it at least once.

Sparks ignite the priming powder.

The pan cover is attached to the frizzen. When the flint strikes, the pan pivots open to expose the priming powder.

Priming powder "flashes" through the touch hole and ignites the powder in the barrel.

SIDELOCK RIFLES

erhaps the most common "traditional" muzzleloader is the sidehammer caplock. These rifles provide the look and the link with the past while maintaining the "modern" performance of a percussion ignition system.

Sidelocks have lost a lot of ground to in-line guns in today's market, but for the most part, any true advantage for the in-line is cosmetic and illusionary. Sidelocks are accurate and dependable—maybe not quite as accurate and dependable as a good in-line—but the difference is so small that it's almost immeasurable. A sidelock looks more like a traditional muzzleloader, and the feel in your hand as you carry one while hunting is unique. I can tell I'm holding a sidelock even when I'm blindfolded.

I feel more like I am muzzleloader hunting when I use a sidelock. It's the gun I started blackpowder hunting with, and those roots run deep. There are unwritten ground rules that are personal and subjective. I believe that a side-lock should have blued or plumb-brown metal, brass fixtures and wood for a stock. However, tastes vary and today's hunter can select stainless steel and a laminated wood or synthetic stock if desired.

The sidelock muzzleloader is so named because the percussion cap is on the side of the barrel. The hammer strikes the cap, which sends ignition fire through to the side of the powder charge.

HOW THEY WORK

What all sidelocks have in common is a large dogleg hammer on the right side of the gun (except for the very rare left-hand models). This hammer is cocked and when the trigger (often double-set triggers) is pulled, the hammer falls to strike a nipple mounted on the side of the rear of the barrel. The strike sets off a percussion cap that

Sidelocks are most popular with hunters who wish to maintain the traditional look and operation of the 18th century muzzleloader rifles.

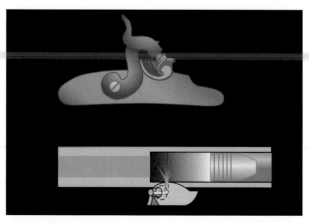

The hammer strikes the cap (top), sending a flame through the ignition channel (bottom) into the powdercharge in the barrel.

has been placed over the nipple and sends a flame through the ignition channel to the side of the powder charge. The powder ignites, launching the bullet.

Some gun enthusiasts argue that igniting the powder from the side is less accurate than lighting the fire from the rear-center. They also argue that the heavy fall of the massive hammer can degrade accuracy by causing the gun to move before the bullet exits. Technically speaking, these arguments are valid but academic at best. Any serious shooter knows that sidelock guns are capable of outstanding accuracy.

What is inarguable about muzzleloaders is that compared to today's stark and pragmatic modern in-line hunting guns, a well designed and executed sidelock muzzleloader has a lot more soul.

Today, many sidelock rifles come in a Hawken format.

HAWKEN RIFLES

While playing Jeremiah Johnson in his early days in the Rocky Mountain wilderness, Robert Redford's primary goal was the procurement of a Hawken rifle. In the mid-1800s, many Western explorers learned that the small-caliber rifles popular in the East were no match for the big game of the West. The scarcity of lead and powder had caused the evolution of highly accurate but minimally powerful guns for the game native to the area where most of the population lived.

These smaller guns worked well on Virginia whitetails if the shot was placed carefully, but the little balls were far too light for elk. Even more important was that even with good shot placement, the little guns usually only made a grizzly mad, which was not a good thing. After quite a few men were killed and a lot more were scarred, it was determined that larger bores were needed in order for those venturing West to survive.

Enter the "Hawken Rifle," a term used to describe the style of rifle made popular by Jacob & Samuel Hawken, the elite gun makers of the time. This short, large-bore rifle soon became recognized as the state-of-the-art big game rifle of that era. With its short barrel, the Hawken was easy to carry on horseback and was fast to load, but most important,

it had a bigger hole down the center of the barrel than most other rifles did at that time. Its larger ball struck a harder blow and penetrated deeper, making it better suited for the largest game in North America.

Jeremiah Johnson finally got his Hawken after prying it from the frozen hands of the carcass that was once a man named "Hatchet Jack." As testimony to the harsh life that mountain men lived, in the will made out to anyone finding him, Jack stated that "It is a good gun and it kilt the bar that kilt me." Although the man had felled the bear with a single shot from the powerful gun, he knew he couldn't survive with the leg the bear had broken before the shot. Jack's high esteem for the rifle was in the will itself: A Hawken was the finest possession a man like him could have.

THE HAWKEN TODAY

Today we don't suffer shortages of powder and lead, but we are strapped with game made scarce and spooky by many generations of disappearing habitat and booming human populations. We also have much less time to hunt, we crave trophy animals when we do hunt, and our demands in terms of rifle performance are not all that far from those of the mountain men. Few of us will ever shoot at enraged grizzly bears with our muzzleloaders, but we also cannot afford to pass on a ten-point buck simply

The Thompson/Center Arms Hawken Rifle is credited with launching the modern muzzleloader revival.

because we couldn't get the perfect shot needed with a sub-caliber muzzleloader.

We cannot ethically accept the possibility of losing wounded game simply because of smaller-bore guns. When hunting big game today with blackpowder, there is no excuse or reason for a small bullet. The low velocity of the coal burners will not cause hydrostatic shock as do the high-speed small bullets of today's firearms.

Instead, a muzzleloader bullet kills by tissue damage from the bullet hole itself, and through hemorrhaging induced by that hole. So it only makes sense that when you poke a hole in a deer with a muzzleloader, it should be a big one—the kind of hole that made the Hawken famous.

THE THOMPSON/CENTER CONNECTION

Thompson/Center Arms is often credited with instigating the modern muzzleloader boom, and the gun it used to initiate this phenomenon was the Hawken Rifle. In the world of modern muzzle-loading for big game, T/C Arms is a name synonymous with replica Hawken rifles.

In 1970, modern muzzleloaders consisted mostly of imported reproductions of dubious quality. The hunting market consisted primarily of a few souls pining for the old ways and wishing they had been born 150 years earlier. T/C Arms was enjoying success with its switch-barrel Contender handgun and was looking for another new and unique firearm to make and market. After looking at the state of the muzzleloader market, T/C Arms decided that blackpowder hunting was an unexplored area that just might resonate with hunters looking for a new challenge.

The Thompson/Center Arms Hawken is available in both caplock and flintlock, as shown here with a very nice white-tail buck.

A study in the contrast of modern muzzleloaders, the Thompson/Center Hawken sidelock and the bolt-action, in-line Knight DISC Rifle.

T/C Arms speculated that if a high-quality muzzleloader rifle were offered with a package of needed components as well as coherent instructions, it just might prove to be the "better mousetrap" muzzleloading needed. Just to be sure, T/C Arms padded its hands with a lifetime warranty.

Warren Center designed the gun while Jim Sheridan worked on the instructions. The first Thompson/Center Hawken Rifles were shipped in late 1970 and an entire industry was launched.

Today's modern muzzleloader owes a debt of thanks to those visionaries at Thompson/Center Arms who started the "fad" that made this book possible. Without the Hawken rifle, we might not be able to enjoy modern muzzleloader hunting as we know it today. Without the initial mainstream interest generated by the T/C Hawken, I doubt we would have seen the rise of special hunting seasons for muzzleloaders. Nor would we have seen the technology develop that brought us in line guns, replica powders, sabot bullets and fiber-optic sights.

As I see the history of modern muzzleloader hunting, it has all descended from the Thompson/Center Hawken rifle—a remarkable evolution in only a few decades.

IN-LINE MUZZLELOADERS

Anybody who knows me knows that I like to argue. After hunting and shooting, arguing may well be my favorite pastime. Being open-minded and objective, I always acknowledge that there are two sides to every argument: the wrong one, and mine.

But I'll never waste my time in an argument without a point. Take, for example, the perpetual debate about in-line blackpowder rifles. The opposition argues *ad nauseum* about the "unfair advantages" of the in-line over the so-called "traditional" muzzleloaders.

NOT THAT NEW

The in-line design has been around for years. Jean Samuel Pauley used an in-line system in 1812, and the Germans had an in-line flintlock design as early as 1738. So tell me how a sidelock is more "traditional."

Sure, the in-line has some advantages. Faster lock time is one; more positive ignition is another. Both contribute to reliability and accuracy. But if you are careful about the details, any muzzleloader is reliable. And the accuracy advantage for the average shooter under normal hunting conditions is almost immeasurable.

Top shelf modern .50 caliber in-line muzzleloaders. Left to right: Knight MK 95, Muzzleloading Technologies, Inc. Model 97 Whitetail Hunter and Thompson/Center Arms Black Diamond.

Scopes are a little easier to mount on in-lines, but they can be mounted on any muzzleloader with only a little more trouble. And no scope in

A scope on any muzzleloader doesn't make it any more accurate; it simply makes the rifle easier to aim precisely.

the world will make a rifle shoot any better, or bring game in close for a shot. Scopes only make it easier to aim.

NOT THAT DIFFERENT

In-lines are still primitive firearms that load from the muzzle using the same blackpowder or equivalent and firing the same bullets that are used in other muzzleloaders. They are still slow to load, subject to the whims of the weather, and their bullet trajectories still drop like a stone when compared to modern rifle calibers.

No matter what the advertisers and the prosti-

There is nothing like the reliability of a modern in-line muzzleloader to instill confidence in a young hunter.

tuted writers tell you, there is no magic in an in-line that suddenly turns it into a flat-shooting, tack-driving, long-range hunting rifle. The parts important to shooting—the barrel, projectile, powder and loading system—remain and perform basically the same as any muzzleloader.

Muzzleloader manufacturers correctly concluded that if they made the guns look and feel like modern rifles, hunters would be more comfortable buying and using them. Inadvertently, this marketing brilliance created its own controversy. The primary advantage of in-lines is one of perception. With stainless steel and synthetic materials coupled with styling that copies modern rifles, they somehow seem to be "more advanced" than other muzzleloaders and so must be "unfair" to use.

Considering the real enemies we face as muzzleloader hunters and shooters these days, this seems a foolish reason to fight among ourselves. I think the best way to negate the argument is to say, "You use what you like and I'll use what I like, as long as we both stuff the bullets in the front." Let's work together to ensure that we and our children will be able to do the same in the years ahead.

TODAY'S IN-LINES

In-lines dominate the muzzleloader hunting market today, and their sales far outpace traditional sidelock guns. Much of that popularity exists because in-lines look and feel like the guns we have used all our lives. We like the way in-lines look and feel, so we buy them. Later, we like them because we see they are very accurate, thanks primarily to quality manufacturing processes and good triggers more than anything inherent to the design.

In-lines dominate the muzzleloader hunting market today, and sales far outpace traditional sidelock guns.

Most in-lines also use fast twist barrels designed for sabot bullets, which adds more to the rifles' reputation for accuracy and performance.

The better in-line guns are manufactured on CNC computer-controlled machines that hold tight tolerances. The guns come with high-quality barrels and crisp, clean triggers. The common synthetic stocks provide a consistency in bedding, and it all adds up to excellent accuracy.

Most in-lines also use fast twist barrels designed for sabot bullets, which further adds to the in-line's reputation for accuracy and performance. If you consider this plus the better ignition performance (the darn thing goes off more often), you can start to understand why so many hunters use in-lines.

How They Work

The most common in-line rifles use a massive bolt that slides inside the receiver. This bolt is held back against spring pressure when the gun is cocked. Pulling the trigger releases the bolt and moves it forward to strike the percussion cap fitted on a nipple that is screwed into the rear of the barrel.

The travel of the bolt in an in-line is relatively short and quick compared to the long hammer fall of a sidelock gun. Consequently, an in-line's lock time (the time between when the trigger is pulled and when the gun fires) is faster than a sidelock's. Also, with the shorter and straighter path the ignition fire travels to the powder, the gun fires quicker. The advantage of a fast lock time is that there is less time for the sights to wander off the target in the moment between when the shooter pulls the trigger and when the gun fires. This is a big advantage for target shooters, but for close-range blackpowder hunting, its value is subject to some debate.

One big in-line advantage I mentioned is that the "fire" from the ignition system has a straight line of travel to reach the back of the powder column. This is slightly faster, and uses less of the

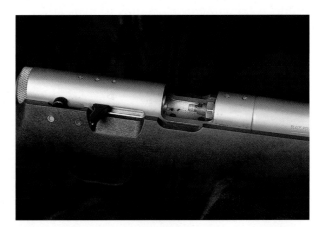

The travel of the bolt in an in-line is relatively short and quick. Also, with the shorter and straighter line of travel that the ignition fire travels to the powder, the gun fires quicker.

In-Line Challenges

One problem with in-lines is that with the tight tolerances between the bolt and receiver combined with a relatively weak hammer strike, any retarding of the bolt movement can result in misfires. With the open-receiver design that most in-lines have, snow, ice, dirt, debris or powder fouling can build up in the receiver. It doesn't take much before it affects performance. Most in-line shooters know enough to disassemble the gun to clean and lubricate it before starting any hunt, but more than one has been surprised when snow or ice built up during the hunt and the gun failed to fire.

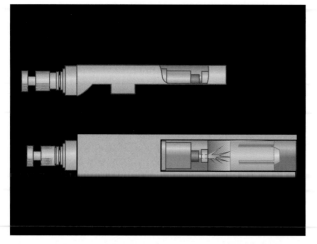

The bolt releases, striking and igniting cap or primer (top). That fire travels straight through the ignition channel to the waiting powder charge (bottom).

ignition power to reach the powder column. The result? A hotter flame remaining to light the powder.

With a sidelock ignition, the "fire" comes in to the side of the powder column and, in many designs, the fire must also make a turn or two through the ignition channel, all of which consumes energy. The in-line approach results in more positive ignition and a cleaner burn of the powder. Using Pyrodex, which has a much higher ignition temperature than blackpowder, can prevent the annoying hang fires so common to sidelocks. (A hang fire is when you can clearly hear the cap go off before the gun actually fires.)

There might also be some credence to the idea that lighting the powder column from the center-rear rather than from the side gives a better burn and is more accurate. This rear ignition also is important to the use of Pyrodex pellets, which were developed for use in in-line rifles and require the ignition to come from the rear.

But in terms of pure hunting effectiveness, the modern in-line is the clear choice for today's modern blackpowder hunter.

In terms of pure hunting effectiveness, the modern in-line is the clear choice for today's modern blackpowder hunter.

BOLT-ACTION IN-LINE MUZZLELOADERS

*I*t was snowing, almost too hard, and it was tough to see because of both the snow-filled air and the wind that was driving it into my face. My eyes watered as I strained to pick out the right track. As I crossed the open field, the wind and snow were filling the tracks almost too fast for me to continue following them, so I was pleased when the trail turned and headed into the thick woods.

In the woods, protected from the wind, the soft, deep snow showed the tracks as if they were from a laser printer. The trouble was that there were too many deer making them. Sorting out the tracks was slow and tedious work. It took total concentration, which was hard to maintain because of fatigue. When I slipped past the big old hemlock tree, it took me a second to realize that the tracks I was following had made a hard turn left.

A brown blur inside an explosion of flying snow snapped my attention to where the deer had been bedded beside the hemlock just a few yards from me. I swung the rifle and, putting a cloud of white smoke into the air, made history in a small sort of way.

The folks at Remington later told me that was the first whitetail ever taken with the new Model 700 Muzzleloader rifle. Actually, it was a joint effort. Earlier that day, an inexperienced member of our party had hit the deer. Our host was color blind and unable to see the blood trail, so it fell on me to track and find the wounded deer. When I finally did, it presented a tough shooting situation, but the Remington felt comfortable in my hands. Because it was a Model 700, it was as familiar as my boots while deer hunting. I don't even recall looking through the Leupold scope, but I know I did because the Barnes MZ Expander (also new at the time) took out the lungs. That kind of instinctive shooting is only possible with a familiar gun that fits the shooter well.

The Remington MZ-700 Bolt Action Muzzleloader was the first bolt-action muzzleloader.

The first whitetail taken with the Remington MZ-700 Muzzleloader was shot during a Vermont snowstorm.

A Bolt-Action Oddysey

In the next few months, I carried the rifle on several long, tough days spent hunting whitetails and hogs. It never failed in conditions ranging from a New England "nor'easter" blizzard, to 100°F Texas heat, to the rain and humidity of south Florida. I suppose that year I walked 100 miles or more while carrying this rifle, and I shot at game from that running deer up close to a trotting coyote at nearly 200 yards. (I am humbled to say I missed that coyote. It was no fault of the gun; I misjudged the distance and singed his belly hair.) The gun accounted for a bunch of game. I emptied more than a few cans of powder on the range while testing several bullets and powders with it. In short, during that hunting season, I shot the Remington Model 700 Muzzleloader (MZ) enough to have formed some opinions.

I like it a lot. But then it's a Remington 700; I've always liked them.

Feel & Familiarity

This muzzleloader looks, handles and feels just like the most popular bolt-action rifle of all time. Because it does, it has started another mini-revolution in modern muzzleloader hunting. Back when the Remington bolt-action muzzleloader was first introduced, in-line rifles were dominating the market. It would have made sense to take that approach and develop a new in-line rifle design. Remington, though, banked on the name recognition and long-term appeal of their Model 700 bolt-action rifle.

There is something to be said for familiarity and the comfort it brings, because the Model 700 MZ was an unprecedented success. It brought a lot

of folks who may not have otherwise tried the sport into the muzzleloading fraternity. After all, hunters had been using Model 700 rifles for years; now they could expand into blackpowder hunting and stay with a gun they knew well.

How It Works

The action on the Remington is a modified short-action 700 with the bolt cocking on opening just like any 700. But there are some differences.

The bolt features a modified firing pin protruding from the open face of the shortened bolt and a cup on the end. When firing, this cup moves forward to strike the cap on the nipple to fire the rifle. The cup also serves to direct any gases escaping from the nipple forward and away from the shooter.

The bolt lacks the twin front lugs that turn and lock into the rear of the barrel on a conventional bolt action. The lugs are not necessary, as the bolt doesn't bear any pressure when firing. Instead of these locking forward lugs to hold the bolt in place when closed, the Remington has a heavy screw that threads through the rear section of the action and fits into a slot milled into the bolt. This slot is milled parallel with the bolt to allow it to be drawn back to place a cap on the nipple. (While a capping tool is helpful, this is one of the few in-line rifles that can be capped with your fingers with relative ease.)

Then as the bolt is pushed forward, the slot turns upward in a two-step angle to cam against the screw and turn the bolt handle down. This duplicates the feel of a regular two-lug bolt action and locks the bolt into position. Gone also is the standard bolt release. To remove the bolt, you simply back off on the screw until it clears the slot and releases the bolt.

Bolt-action muzzleloaders are now a big part of the modern muzzleloading scene. The author shot this Iowa buck with a Knight DISC Rifle.

More Advantages

The lock time of this action is an incredibly fast 3.0 milliseconds, partly because of the very short movement of the striker. Accuracy is enhanced in a couple of ways. First is the short lock time important to any accurate firearm. Second is the short striker travel, which does not disturb the rifle with the movement that a longer striker travel creates.

It might be argued that bolt actions (top) are nothing more than in-line muzzleloaders, but there are some clear differences.

The barrel is threaded for a removable stainless steel breach plug. The nipple then threads into the breach plug. By removing the nipple and then the breach plug, you can clean the bore from the rear. This also ensures a complete cleaning job, necessary to any blackpowder gun but imperative with an in-line.

Fouling can build up in the action of any in-line and impede the striker until the gun fails to fire, so it is important to disassemble the rifle and clean it completely, although the Remington 700 MZ design is as close to immune from this as any in-line I have tested. Its moving parts inside the bolt are more protected from fouling than most in-lines.

Like all Remington Model 700 guns, the MZ is extremely accurate. The single best 100-yard group I have ever fired with a muzzleloader was with that first Remington 700 MZ, using a Barnes 300-grain Sabot MZ Expander Copper bullet and 100 grains of Goex FFg blackpowder. The cap was a #11 CCI. Three shots were within six-tenths of an inch, center to center.

A Simple Solution

The concept of a bolt-action muzzleloader took off and it seems like just about every gun maker has a bolt-action muzzleloader in its catalog. They are a big part of the modern muzzleloading scene, and it's a safe bet they are here to stay.

It might be argued that bolt actions are nothing more than in-line muzzleloaders, and to a point this is true. Certainly bolt actions use the same in-line configuration in the ignition system and barrel. The difference is in the firing mechanism. The moving parts are housed inside the bolt mechanism and as a result, they are protected from fouling and weather-induced drag on the bolt. As a rule, bolt-action muzzleloaders also have a faster lock time. Lock time is the lag from when the trigger is pulled to when the gun fires. It is generally accepted that the faster the lock time, the more accuracy the gun will display when fired by anything other than a machine rest.

A bolt-action muzzleloader also has less mass in the moving parts as it fires. The more the mass, the greater the disturbance caused when the bolt strikes the cap. Most in-line rifles use a massive sliding bolt that moves to strike the firing cap, but a bolt action uses a much lighter-weight internal striker.

The downside is that the bolt must be disassembled and cleaned after every shooting session. The single most common reason that bolt-action muzzleloaders are returned for repairs is that the bolts were not properly cleaned.

CVA, Knight, Remington, Ruger, Savage, Traditions and many other companies offer bolt-action muzzleloaders. Bolt actions are a huge part of the muzzleloader hunting market these days and might well be the preferred action of choice for a serious hunter in-the-know about modern muzzleloader performance.

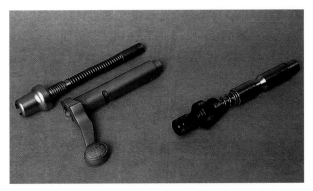

The moving parts are of a bolt-action muzzleloader are housed inside the bolt mechanism and protected from fouling and weather-induced drag on the bolt. Shown is a disassembled Remington bolt (left) beside an in-line bolt.

The Early Days with the Remington Model 700 MZ

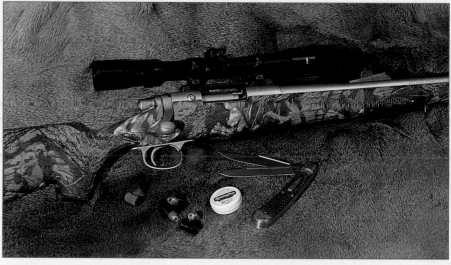

The Remington MZ-700 Muzzleloader.

After shooting that Vermont whitetail mentioned earlier, I took the Model 700 MZ on a cross-country hunting odyssey.

February found me in Texas, where an exciting and grueling chase ended with the dogs baying up a large hog. It was Dr. Chuck DeNunzio's turn to shoot, so I handed the Remington to him, but he had to wait. Under that mesquite tree was an ill-defined ball of hog and dogs writhing and undulating and offering no certain target.

The legendary Texas hog guide, "Barefoot Bob," doesn't look kindly on Yankees who shoot his dogs, so it was prudent to wait. Finally an opening appeared, and at the shot, the hog dropped in its tracks and never wiggled. Both the dogs and Bob stared in amazement—even the good doctor was a little surprised—but I expected nothing less from the Remington.

I took that gun to South Florida to hunt hogs on the Seminole Indians' Big Cypress reservation. The place is simply "Hog Heaven" with more pork-on-the-hoof than I have ever seen in one location. I took two blackpowder hogs in as many shots, and folks I loaned the rifle to took three more. The only thing anybody who tries this rifle asks is, "Where can I get one?"

The Model 700 MZ showed a definite preference for sabot bullets in general and the new Barnes Expander MZ solid-copper bullets in particular. That season, I used the 300-grain version to take two deer and two wild hogs. The same type of bullet also accounted for four more hogs shot by

Dr. Chuck DeNunzio took this Texas hog with one of the first Remington Model 700 MZ Muzzleloaders.

others with the Remington. Only one bullet was recovered. (One actually hit a smallish whitetail head-on and penetrated the full length to exit on the hip.)

That single recovered bullet hit a large boar hog in the left shoulder and was found embedded in the thick cartilage shield on the right shoulder. It had to be cut out with a knife, and had this been a critter without the thick shield common only to a boar hog, there's no doubt that the bullet would also have exited. The bullet showed classic six-petal expansion to .950, and 100 percent weight retention.

Time and again this rifle amazed me when I shot it from a bench rest. I took it to Texas on a varmint/hog hunt, and when we were sighting in at the range, I turned in better groups than some of the hunters who shot centerfire rifles.

A few years ago, my daughter took her first deer on the last day of the Vermont muzzleloader season. Erin, then 12, made me proud as she managed to stay cool under a tough high-pressure situation and put a Nosler 250-grain

The Barnes 300-grain .50 Expander-MZ bullet. The expanded bullet was recovered from a wild hog.

Partition bullet through the deer's lungs. It may not be the biggest deer on earth, and in fact she has taken several larger in the recent seasons, but there is only one first deer in any hunter's lifetime. That she took hers with a muzzleloader made it even more memorable.

Chasing hogs is hunting fun, pure and simple. A muzzleloader makes it even more exciting! This bruiser fell to a Remington Model 700 MZ on the Seminole reservation in South Florida.

Twelve-year-old Erin Towsley with her first deer. First deer are very special. That she took hers with a muzzleloader (in this case a Remington MZ) made it even more memorable.

THE OTHER MUZZLELOADERS

There are some muzzleloaders that simply don't fit into an existing category. Some are innovative, some are not. Some work well, some do not. Some are illegal in places, most are not. They are, however, all viable modern muzzle hunting tools.

I doubt anybody knows about every single one. There are simply too many basement inventors developing guns. It would be impossible to keep up with them all and still claim to have a life. There are a few, however, that I have used and am familiar with.

MOSSBERG MODEL 500 SHOTGUN BARREL

If you own one of the ubiquitous Mossberg Model 500 12 gauge pump-action shotguns (and who doesn't?), there is an inexpensive way to start muzzleloader hunting. Mossberg offers a 24-inch, .50 caliber replacement barrel with a 1:26 inch twist rate (for more information on twist rates, see pages 48–50).

The barrel simply replaces the shotgun barrel. Changing takes only a couple of minutes and requires no special tools. The breech plug is fitted for a #209 shotgun primer and when the slide is pulled forward, the bolt locks against the rear of the barrel, positioning the firing pin to

The Mossberg Model 500 Shotgun with a .50 caliber muzzleloader barrel installed.

strike the primer. When the gun is pumped to open the action, an ejector pulls the primer out of the breech plug so it can be easily removed. The breech is well protected from the weather.

With the barrel, you get a replacement end cap for the magazine tube. It has a hole through the center to accept the synthetic ramrod. The ferrule on the end of the rod is threaded to screw into a guide that's welded to the end of the barrel. This keeps the ramrod in place and ensures against loss. The barrel comes fitted either with fully adjustable Williams fiberoptic sights or with standard rifle sights. Most Model 500 shotguns of recent vintage are drilled and tapped for scope mounting.

The Mossberg Model 500 shotgun uses a 209 shotgun primer with its muzzleloader barrel. The primer can be seen inside the open action.

The Cabela's Kodiak Express Double Rifle.

CABELA'S DOUBLE GUN

I have always loved double guns. I grew up shooting side-by-side shotguns, and my interest in Africa has always drawn me to double rifles (although my bank account keeps sucking me back away from them!). So how can I not like the Cabela's Kodiak Express Double Rifle Muzzleloader? How can anybody not like it?

The trouble with any double rifle is regulating the barrels to strike at the same point of impact. It is probably the single most relevant reason for the extremely high cost. This gun uses a unique approach. It has two flip-up rear sights, one for each barrel. How wonderfully simple.

Cabela's Kodiak Express Double Rifle has a sight for each barrel. They are designed to pivot up or down for individual use.

Where it's legal, having a second shot is something that most muzzleloader hunters I know have wished for at least a few times in their hunting careers.

CABELA'S ROLLING BLOCK

The "other" blackpowder rifles that are growing in popularity are blackpowder cartridge guns. I enjoy shooting and hunting with my Navy Arms Remington Rolling Block reproduction gun in .45-70 Gov. I load it with 400-grain cast bullets and 70 grains of Goex cartridge-

The Cabela's Rolling Block Muzzleloader Rifle.

grade blackpowder. My gun has taken bears and harvested lots and lots of targets.

Cabela's offers several proprietary muzzleloader guns. One that I find interesting is a muzzleloader rifle that uses a timeless rolling-block design. To use it, the hammer is cocked and the action opened by pulling on a wing that opens or "rolls" the breech block back.

The breech plug is fitted to take a musket cap. Close the breechblock and the gun is ready to fire. If you are not ready, simply lower the hammer to the half-cock position. The .50 caliber gun has a 26½-inch barrel with a 1:24 twist and is rated for 3-pellet, 150-grain charges.

It comes supplied with fiber-optic sights and is drilled and tapped for mounting a scope. It is also offered as a package deal with a scope already installed.

The Cabela's Rolling Block Muzzleloader Rifle with the Navy Arms Rolling Block Rifle in .45-70. Both are based on the old Remington Rolling Block Rifle from the 19th century.

The Markesbery "Outer-Line" Muzzleloader rifle uses a unique in-line ignition angle.

MARKESBERY "OUTER-LINE"

This gun barely makes the cut for this category. It's pretty much an "in-line" gun. But the Markesbery brothers who make it like to call it an "Outer-Line" ignition system. This rear ignition system has the nipple turned up at a 45-degree angle. An external hammer strikes the nipple and fires the gun. Markesbery's most interesting ignition system is the 400 SRP Magnum Ignition System, which uses a small-rifle #400 primer in a closed system that has a screw-on cap.

The Markesbery "Outer-Line" Muzzleloader rifle can use a small rifle primer in a closed system that protects it from the elements.

There are several configurations available in the gun. They all feature interchangeable barrels. Mine has a thumbhole and a two-piece laminated wood stock.

PRAIRIE RIVER ARMS "BULLPUP"

This gun would have a die-hard traditionalist foaming at the mouth and drooling on his buckskins! "Different" hardly even comes close to a fair description.

The "bullpup" design has the barrel and/or action set well back into the stock. It results in a very short gun with an odd sort of balance. The concept is most often employed in fighting guns, the idea being that a shorter gun is quicker to maneuver and presents less for the opponent to grab. But the idea of using the design in a hunting gun is less farfetched than a first look might imply.

One of the most unique muzzleloaders on the market today is the Prairie River Arms "Bullpup."

When hunting in thick brush or from a tight treestand, a short gun is always an asset. Also, anybody who has ever tried to quietly sneak a long-barreled rifle out of a box blind window might know why a short gun is a good idea. I know at least one outstanding 12-point whitetail deer that owes his life to my inability to stick a long object out a blind window without making enough noise to let him know it was a good time to "get the hell out of Dodge."

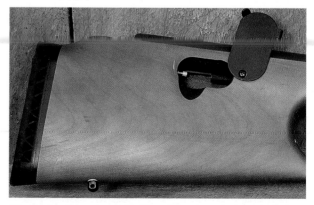

The Prairie River Arms "Bullpup" has its priming nipple in the butt stock. This helps create a rifle that has a very short overall length.

The PRA Bullpup's barrel extends into the stock almost to the rear. It actually forms the comb of the stock and is what the shooter rests his cheek on when shooting. Even though the barrel is 28 inches long, the overall length of the gun is only 32 inches! The nipple is well behind the trigger and faces forward. It is accessed through a port in the right side of the butt stock. The bolt cocks by pulling forward and, when firing, it moves back to strike the nipple behind in the gun.

Because the shooter's face rests on the barrel, the sights must be high. The ramped front sight is about 2.5 inches above the centerline of the barrel. The adjustable rear peep sight sits on a large bracket that also forms a "suitcase-style" handle for carrying the gun. There is a scope mount that easily and quickly attaches to this "handle" with a single bolt with a large knurled knob so no tools are required. This base accepts Weaver-style rings.

A pivoting safety is in front of the trigger; it swings in to fire and out for safety. For the hunter looking for "something different," this gun is "cool." I am planning to hunt with it, and I'll bet it will elicit a comment or two in the whitetail woods!

THOMPSON/CENTER ENCORE

Thompson/Center Arms is a leading manufacturer of muzzleloaders, but for years it has also had a very successful centerfire, switch-barrel handgun and carbine called the Contender.

In 1996, T/C Arms introduced a "big brother" to the Contender called the Encore. This too is a switch-barrel, break-action handgun or rifle that easily changes barrels and calibers. Among the most popular options, one that can be bought as a second barrel for an existing gun or as a complete gun, is a .50 caliber muzzleloader. T/C calls it the 209X50 (because it uses a #209 shotgun primer and is .50 caliber). The 209X50 is one of the strongest, most accurate, reliable and easy-to-use guns on the market.

The bullet and powder are loaded into the .50 caliber barrel just like any other muzzleloader. It's a "magnum" gun, so up to 150-grain charges are acceptable. Pulling on the trigger guard opens the break-action gun and

The Thompson/Center Arms Encore 209X50 Muzzleloader.

exposes the breech plug. This gun is designed to accept a #209 shotgun primer. Pushing up on the barrel closes the gun and pushes the primer into the breech to ensure a tight seal. Cocking the exposed hammer readies the gun to fire.

Sights or the scope are mounted on the barrel so it stays sighted-in when switching barrels. The trigger is very good and because the breech is sealed, water has a hard time finding the powder. Also, with this closed-breech design, all the fouling stays in the barrel. The action is kept fouling-free and cleaning is easy. Like all T/C guns, it has a reputation for accuracy.

You can, of course, also buy centerfire barrels in a variety of chambering or a 20 gauge shotgun barrel in smooth bore or rifled bore. Versatility is a big selling point for this gun.

The Thompson/Center Arms Encore 209X50 Muzzleloader uses a 209 shotgun primer in a closed breech system that protects the primer from weather.

YOUTH GUNS

*I*f you really want to hook your kids onto shooting and hunting, let them shoot muzzleloaders. The intimate and simple closeness to the process is both educational and fun. And what kid doesn't love getting dirty? What's any messier to shoot than blackpowder? If you bring them home with black hands and smudged faces, you know they had a good day of shooting.

Some kids are going to be ready to hunt when they are still physically small. For them, trying to learn to shoot and hunt with "adult-sized" equipment can be frustrating.

Smaller hunters' requirements are a little different from the requirements of the mythical "average" male adult.

Young hunters need a scaled-down gun with a stock that has a shorter length of pull, allowing shorter arms to reach the trigger and smaller eyes to line up in the correct place for sighting. A shorter barrel and overall length makes the gun easier to handle and, of course, lighter guns are easier to carry. A growing number of gun makers are finally recognizing these needs and cataloging "youth" models which actually work and are designed specifically for smaller hunters.

Youth guns left to right: Remington MZ-700 Youth, Knight Wolverine II Youth and CVA Youth Hunter. The yardstick illustrates the shorter length of pull in the stocks designed for smaller shooters.

If you really want to hook your kids on shooting and hunting, let them shoot muzzleloaders.

iber sidelock is a good fit and a good shooter. With a 50-grain charge of FFg and a round ball, the gun's recoil is light. We will increase the charge to a 250-grain Nosler Partition Sabot bullet with 90 grains of powder next hunting season when, after a summer of practice, Nathan has plans to shoot a buck with this gun.

A veteran hunter already, he is prepared for the challenge of hunting with an open-sighted, sidelock gun. But when he and his sister, Erin, started hunting, I had different goals. For the serious business of deer hunting, I wanted to start them both off with muzzleloaders that were familiar in look and feel to their centerfire rifles.

Beginning to hunt can be confusing enough with all a young hunter needs to learn; I didn't want to compound the problem with drastically different equipment. We selected Remington Model 700 ML Youth bolt-action, .50 caliber in-line guns. I mounted 2-7X Nikon scopes and they could see little difference from the Model 700 ADL .243 Win. rifles with the same optics.

That fall, Erin took her first whitetail with that muzzleloader and displayed an ability to handle tough hunting situations. That ability, I might add, has served her well in the past few years on several more successful hunts.

TAKE THEM HUNTING

My goal here is not to plug a specific muzzleloader for youth hunting, but to illustrate that for somebody motivated enough to investigate, there are guns out there that will fit the needs

Our kids are the future of hunting. They are the only hope for our sport to survive.

of your little hunting buddy. These kids are the next generation, they are the future, they are the only hope for our sport to survive. We owe it to them and the sport to help in any way we can.

Besides, you will wind up with a lifelong hunting partner and kids who understand responsibility.

A RIFLE OF THEIR OWN

Ownership of the tools used for shooting and hunting is important to building a sense of belonging. To create a lifelong interest, you must make sure that the kids feel they are an important part of your participation in the sport and not just somebody you allow to tag along as a nuisance to be endured out of some sense of misplaced parental guilt. A big part of that is making sure they have some equipment to call their own. It gives them a sense of permanence, and what singular piece of equipment is more important than the muzzleloader itself?

I am sure that lots of guns suitable for kids are on the market, but I can only comment on those my kids and I have tried. Maybe my experience will help you select the right rifle for your young hunters.

My son, Nathan, loves muzzleloader shooting and prefers the traditional approach of a sidelock. The affordable CVA Youth Hunter .50 cal-

THE NEW SMOKELESS POWDER MUZZLELOADER

The Savage Model 10 ML is capable of shooting with smokeless powder.

In the "it had to happen sooner or later" category, Savage brought out a bolt-action muzzleloader designed for smokeless powder. The new Savage Model 10 ML is highly controversial. "This will get people killed," said one industry leader.

No one questions the Savage gun's safety in cases when it is used as intended. In fact, Savage has duplicated some mistakes that they think might happen with the shooting public. For example, in tests, Savage used double loads of powder or loaded two bullets. In some tests, the gun's barrels bulged a little but remained intact. However, the pressures shot up as high as 126,900 P.S.I.—more than four times the standard pressure of 29,000 P.S.I for this gun with smokeless powder loads, and much higher than any blackpowder gun will generate with proper use.

HOW IT WORKS

The gun uses a steel "cartridge" that will hold a 209 shotgun primer. This is inserted into the "chamber" of the specially modified barrel. The bolt closes, forcing it against the machined chamber to seal the gases. The 209 fires through this steel cartridge to ignite the powder charge. The powder and bullet are loaded from the muzzle like any other muzzleloader. The gun will use all blackpowder and blackpowder-substitutes as well as pellets, but it is the only muzzleloader that is also designed for use with smokeless powder.

Smokeless powder obviously works, as velocity and accuracy are good. The best thing in the minds of many shooters is the lack of corrosive fouling, and the easy cleanup. One test report says that the gun gets very fussy in terms of accuracy and is

While smokeless powder should never be used in any other muzzleloader, the Savage Model 10 ML is capable of using either blackpowder or smokeless powder.

demanding with sabot construction as well as powder charge weights. That same report said that with a loose-fitting sabot (which was used most often in testing), the 209 shotgun primer would sometimes blow the powder and bullet forward in the barrel without igniting it. If the shooter were simply to load another primer without reseating the bullet and if the powder were to ignite, the bullet could become an obstruction in the bore with catastrophic results.

Smokeless powder has little of the inherent forgiveness that blackpowder possesses. It is sensitive to very small changes in charge weights and often the addition of only a grain or even less will cause pressures to spike dramatically. Smokeless powder has traditionally been used only for reloading cartridges under controlled conditions. If it is used in a muzzleloader that is designed for it under conditions that are equally controlled, then likely no problems will occur.

A Powder Keg Waiting to Explode, or the Next Step in Muzzleloader Evolution?

But everything that has been drilled into muzzleloader shooters for years sets the stage for an accident. First off, it has always been the standard, printed on every gun and in every owner's manual, never to use smokeless powder in any muzzleloader. If we start to bend that rule, isn't it only a matter of time before somebody loads smokeless in his muzzleloader because he watched his buddy using it in his gun? Or what if he just grabs the

wrong can of powder on his way out the door? Or what if he decides to use a "magnum load" of 150 grains of powder? The autopsy X-rays will show that the breech plug got almost total penetration into his brain.

It has also always been taught that blackpowder and all its substitutes should be measured by volume, not by weight. Every substitute on the market is formulated to be used volume-for-volume with blackpowder. While we express load data in "grains," that applies only to blackpowder itself. While 100 grains of blackpowder should weigh 100 grains on a scale, the equal volume of Pyrodex will weigh less. However, if it is measured by volume so that the volume is exactly the same as 100 grains of blackpowder, the performance level will be the same.

Smokeless powder must always be weighed and never dispensed by volume. Because smokeless powders each use a different weight and volume measure, the potential is very high for a serious problem to occur because a shooter followed the well-established procedures of loading his muzzleloader by volume.

Reactions & Predictions

What do the powder companies say?

"We don't recommend smokeless powder be used in any muzzleloader. That's always been our position and we are not going to change it," said Hodgdon's Chris Hodgdon.

Alliant Powder's Pete Jackson says of smokeless powder, "We recognize that this is the next advancement in muzzleloader technology. We also recognize that our powders will be used in these guns and it's important to remember that all muzzleloader guns, except the Savage, currently should never be used with anything except blackpowder or its substitutes. But if progress allows better performance, we do not discourage that. We feel this is a firearms issue, not a propellant issue. We also agree that there is a concern for the propensity of a lot of confusion and that needs to be addressed."

Finally there is the social question: Will some states use this as a launchpad to attack muzzleloader technology through regulation? Will this open the Pandora's box of legislation and regulation and result in losing hard-fought ground in what's legal and accepted for hunting during muzzleloader seasons? Or is the Savage smokeless powder muzzleloader the forerunner of the next wave of muzzleloader hunting technology? Nobody can say for sure, but it certainly will be interesting.

Chapter 2

MUZZLELOADER BULLETS

*I*n hunting camps throughout the world, the technical aspects of muzzleloader performance are endlessly debated, but perhaps the most misunderstood and misinformed subject of these debates centers on the bullets we use. Bullet selection is a topic inundated with misinformation and myths.

That's unfortunate, because once the bullet exits the barrel, the rest becomes moot. The only physical connection the modern muzzleloader hunter has with the game he is hunting is the bullet. Because of that, the bullet, and the bullet alone, is the final word on the outcome of the hunt. If it was selected with care and does its job as it was designed, things will turn out as planned. But hunters who use the wrong bullet, usually for the wrong reasons, discover that disappointment may follow.

The bullet is, at first glance, a simple lump of metal. In years past, when lead was the only material used, that may well have been true. But the modern muzzleloader's bullets have grown complex and technically advanced. This, of course, has boosted performance, but at the same time it has placed greater demands on the bullets. Designs are targeted to a specific function, and today's muzzleloader bullets are entering into the realm of "niche" bullets aimed at very specific functions.

Until now, the informed hunter has never had the opportunity to launch such advanced bullets from a muzzleloader. But the other end of the spectrum is that the uninformed or misinformed hunter has never had as great a potential for catastrophic failure.

ROUND BALLS

A simple round ball is the oldest rifle projectile that is still in use today. Dating back to the invention of guns themselves, around 1350 A.D., the round ball has existed a lot more years than the latest, high-tech, bonded-core, alloy-jacketed, polymer-tipped bullet can claim in the way of historical value.

Most of today's round balls are used by muzzle-loader hunters who consider themselves traditionalists, or in the few localities that still restrict hunters to them by law.

A simple round ball dates to the invention of guns themselves, back around 1350 A.D., and is the oldest rifle projectile that is still in use today.

ROUND BALL BASICS

Typically, the ball is sized a little smaller than the bore of the rifle. It is then wrapped in a lubricated patch, usually cloth. This patch holds the ball tightly in the bore and mates with the rifling to allow it to impart a spin on the ball as it passes through the bore. This is the same concept as a

Typically the ball is wrapped in a lubricated patch, usually cloth.

sabot and, in reality, the patched round ball was the first sabot bullet used in muzzleloaders.

The round ball should be made of pure lead so that when it is fired, it can obturate and tightly fill the bore, sealing the propellant gases. Harder lead alloy balls do not do this as well and tend not to be as accurate. (Hornady makes hard round balls called "Hard Balls" that use a special plastic sabot rather than a cloth patch. Accuracy is maintained because the sabot seals the bore and the hard balls are said to penetrate better than soft lead.)

Round balls shoot best in guns that are designed for them and that are made with slow twist rates and deep-cut rifling. Round balls are the lightest bullet that can be made in a given caliber and, because of their light weight, will generate higher velocities than conical bullets.

SOME SHORTCOMINGS

But the round ball has trouble hanging on to what it has. Ballistically speaking, the round ball acts like it was designed by a committee, and from a technical standpoint, the round ball is a poor excuse for a bullet.

its flight.

Round balls have a very low ballistic coefficient (BC), which is the measure of how well a bullet overcomes air resistance and retains its velocity and energy downrange. For example, a .490-inch round ball designed to be used in a .50 caliber muzzleloader has a BC of only .067, compared to the Hornady Great Plains full caliber conical 410-grain FP bullet with a BC of .205, almost triple. What this means in the real world is this: If they both start out at a velocity of 1,500 fps, the round ball will travel at 954 fps at 100 yards, while the Great Plains bullet will

You don't need to wear fringed buckskin and leather boots to shoot round balls. Many hunters use them for the tradition and for the romance ... and for the challenge, because you'll want to get closer when you're using round balls. Use a large caliber rifle too, for maximum killing power.

During the internal ballistics process—what happens inside the gun—is when round ball problems begin to rear their ugly head.

The problem starts with the small contact area with the barrel. Because of the radius of a round ball, only a small portion actually grips the rifling and bore to seal gases and steer the bullet. If the twist is too fast or the attempted velocity too high, the result can be the "stripping" of the rifling: The bullet loses its grip and strips enough material off to allow the bullet to pass through the bore in a straight-line direction.

Accuracy is a no-show in this situation. The faster the rifling twist, the shallower the rifling and the higher the velocity, and the more that stripping is apt to occur.

The other side of the equation is that the ball must obturate and fill the rifling enough to seal the bore. If the rifling is too deep or the powder charge too low, this may not occur and gas will leak around the ball at the base of the rifling grooves. This creates not only loss of both accuracy and velocity, but also potential damage to the rifle.

IN THE AIR

Moving on to external ballistics, let's look at what happens to the bullet in the air. It's undeniable that a round ball can be accurate, but that's about the only good thing that can be said about

move along at 1,296 fps.

The energy figures show even greater contrast. The heavier conical bullet starts out with 2,049 foot-pounds of energy while our pathetic round ball has only 875 foot-pounds. This is less than the long-accepted deer hunting standard of 1,000 foot-pounds of energy at the target. At 100 yards, the conical has 1,396 foot-pounds of energy while the round ball is wimping out at 354 foot-pounds.

Even if we boost the muzzle velocity of the round ball to 1,900 fps, which is a common velocity for hunting, it still can't hold up its end of the deal. The round ball starts out with 1,403 foot-pounds of energy, but when it reaches 50 yards, it has only 769 foot-pounds of energy, less than the accepted minimum for deer hunting. At 100 yards, it has dropped to 457 foot-pounds.

PENETRATION & EXPANSION

Finally there is the matter of terminal ballistics, which involves what happens inside the critter you shoot. A round ball cannot be depended on to reliably expand within tissue, but don't be so sure you want it to. If it does expand, it will grow wider than it is long. With this shape, it will probably not penetrate in a straight line like a "regular" bullet will, and it certainly will not penetrate very far. On the other hand, a round ball that retains its shape tends to stretch tissue around its leading edge before breaking through, resulting in a smaller wound cavity than the actual bullet diameter.

The other factor in penetration is a bullet's sectional density (SD), basically a measure of the bullet's weight relative to its diameter. The higher the SD, the better a bullet will penetrate with all else equal. Our .490-inch round ball has an SD of .106 while the Great Plains conical has an SD of .226. It doesn't take a rocket scientist to guess which one will penetrate better.

CREATING ROUND BALLS

Two types of round balls are commonly used these days. Most commercial round balls are cold-swaged under pressure. This results in perfectly round balls with few voids and, of course, no sprue points.

But many shooters prefer to cast their own round balls. This is easy, fun to do and will save money. Careful casting technique and a quality mold will result in round balls with no voids, but any cast bullet will have a sprue. This results from the point where the lead is poured into the mold. A plate called the sprue plate swings on a pivot on one corner to cover the top of the mold. There is a hole through this plate into which the melted lead

Cast round balls will have a sprue point, which must be aligned with the bore on loading. Swaged round balls do not have a sprue.

is poured. After the lead hardens, the sprue plate is hit with a mallet to cut off the lead that is in the pour channel. This leaves a small nib of lead called the sprue. The conventional wisdom is to orient this nib at the top of the ball when loading. This keeps it in line with the axis as the ball spins in flight so it doesn't upset the balance of the bullet.

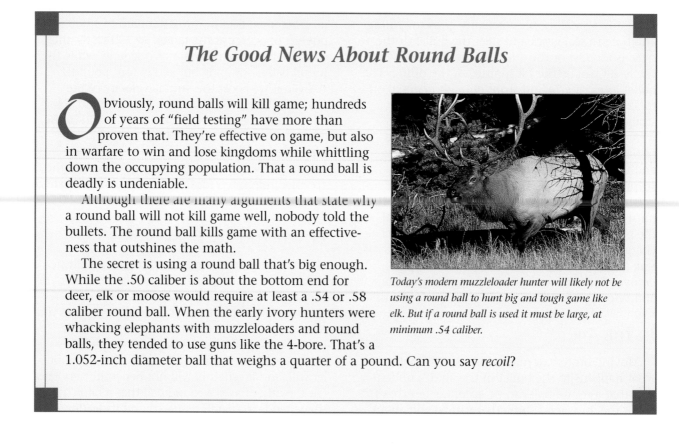

The Good News About Round Balls

Obviously, round balls will kill game; hundreds of years of "field testing" have more than proven that. They're effective on game, but also in warfare to win and lose kingdoms while whittling down the occupying population. That a round ball is deadly is undeniable.

Although there are many arguments that state why a round ball will not kill game well, nobody told the bullets. The round ball kills game with an effectiveness that outshines the math.

The secret is using a round ball that's big enough. While the .50 caliber is about the bottom end for deer, elk or moose would require at least a .54 or .58 caliber round ball. When the early ivory hunters were whacking elephants with muzzleloaders and round balls, they tended to use guns like the 4-bore. That's a 1.052-inch diameter ball that weighs a quarter of a pound. Can you say *recoil*?

Today's modern muzzleloader hunter will likely not be using a round ball to hunt big and tough game like elk. But if a round ball is used it must be large, at minimum .54 caliber.

There is a certain romance in hunting with traditional equipment, including round ball bullets, and any animal taken in such a way is a true trophy. This Wisconsin doe fell to a 230-grain, hand-cast round ball shot from a .54 caliber plains-style rifle.

Round Ball Weights

Bullet Diameter	Bullet Weight
.350	64 grains
.375	80 grains
.433	120 grains
.440	128 grains
.445	133 grains
.451	138 grains
.454	141 grains
.457	144 grains
.490	177 grains
.495	182 grains
.530	224 grains
.535	230 grains
.570	278 grains

THE ROMANCE OF ROUND BALLS

While there is no technical reason to load your hunting rifle with a round ball, the appeal of hunting with this bullet is in the tradition of using the bullets that started with the guns. Somehow shooting a buck with a bonded-core, high-tech, computer-designed, gilding metal-jacketed, alloy-core bullet in a colored technical polymer sabot doesn't carry the same romance as making venison with a round ball nestled in a linen patch.

FULL CALIBER CONICAL BULLETS

The full caliber conical is another bullet design that's been around for a long time. In simple terms, it is the elongated version of the round ball: still bore diameter, but much longer. This allows the weight to be increased and the bearing surface on the rifling to be lengthened. Also, the longer, heavier bullet spins on a central axis, which creates a single leading edge for the bullet in flight.

A conical will retain its velocity and energy better downrange and will penetrate better. Because it has a long shank, the conical can expand and still have the bulk of the bullet behind it, pushing and steering it as it penetrates.

CONICAL ADVANTAGES

Bullet design, weight and maximum velocity are the only variables within a given bore diameter. A conical bullet and a round ball are basically the same diameter in a given muzzleloader caliber. But the .50 caliber round ball will weigh 175 grains, while a conical can be any reasonable weight needed. A conical bullet can easily double or even triple the weight of a round ball in the same bore size.

Of course, being lighter, the round ball will be going a little faster. But with the limitations of blackpowder, the ball's extra speed is not enough to make a big difference in terminal performance.

Because the conical design allows bullet weight to increase within a given bore diameter, energy will increase. A conical bullet can achieve nearly the same velocity as a round ball when used in a blackpowder muzzleloader. But with much higher weight, the conical is far more powerful.

Let's consider momentum. This measurement does not

Because the conical design allows bullet weight to increase within a given bore diameter, energy will increase.

have the velocity bias that energy does, and it gives equal importance to both weight and velocity. This is likely the most accurate measure of the power of a muzzleloader bullet.

At 1,500 fps muzzle velocity, the .490 round ball weighing 175 grains has a momentum factor of 37.5 lb-f/s. The Hornady .50 caliber 410-grain Great Plains bullet at the same velocity has a

Conical bullets come in a variety of styles and designs.

Various bullets recovered from game. Left to right: Full conical .50 caliber; .50 caliber jacketed used in a sabot in a .54 caliber gun; 300-grain Barnes Expander-MZ used in a sabot and .50 caliber gun; and 325-grain Barnes Expander-MZ used in a sabot and .54 caliber gun.

momentum factor of 87.9 lb-f/s, more than 2.3 times greater. At 100 yards, the round ball has a momentum factor of 23.9 lb-f/s, while the conical bullet's factor is 72.5 lb-f/s. This is more than three times greater, so the conical is gaining in its advantage as the distance increases. This becomes even more pronounced as the range increases.

As demonstrated earlier, a conical bullet will have a much higher ballistic coefficient (BC) than any round ball. The exact BC will vary with bullet weight and shape, but it will always be higher than a round ball, and any conical bullet will retain its velocity and energy downrange with

more efficiency than the round ball. With all else being equal, the conical bullet will shoot flatter and hit harder than a round ball at all ranges.

TAKING CARE OF BUSINESS

Finally, we come to terminal ballistics. A well-made conical bullet will have a blunt leading edge that will tend to punch and cut through tissue. This makes a wound channel that's at least as large as the bullet. It may also be designed to expand, increasing the frontal diameter and creating even larger wound channels.

With the increased weight, greater length and higher sectional density, the non-expanding conical will always out-penetrate a round ball. Even an expanding conical will usually still penetrate much deeper than a round ball … as well as cause a lot more tissue damage.

DESIGN & CONSTRUCTION DETAILS

Conical bullets are designed to be full caliber and are not wrapped with a patch or sabot. They are designed to work in different ways. Some, like the Gonic Bullet, simply engrave the rifling when starting into the barrel. Others will taper from bore diameter at the base to groove diameter in the front of the bullet. This allows the smaller base to

When hunting very large game like moose with a muzzleloader, a full caliber conical bullet is one of the best choices.

A full caliber conical bullet is a good choice for any big game hunting.

start into the barrel easily, but the bullet will take the rifling as it expands its diameter closer to the nose of the bullet. Some bullets such as the well-known Thompson/Center Maxi-Ball use larger "driving bands" on the front to accomplish this.

All conicals must be made from soft, pure lead for two reasons. One—so they can easily engrave the rifling when loading. Two—so the bullet can obturate (expand) upon firing, to fill and seal the bore. If they are working correctly, the tapered bullets, or those with front driving bands, will expand to fill the bore the full length of the bullet upon firing.

Some conical designs, such as the Black Belt from Big Bore Express (called the PowerBelt Bullet by CVA, which also sells them) or the PowerPunch from Muzzleloading Technologies, Inc., are actually made to bore diameter or slightly smaller. They do not engrave the rifling when loading, but are designed to obturate and fill the bore to take the shape of the rifling on firing.

These bullets are designed to be used in a fouled bore and are easier to load than a bullet that must scrape through the fouling in the grooves as it's loaded. With these undersized bullets, the fouling actually helps hold them in place until firing.

The Black Belt and PowerBelt bullets feature an attached plastic "wad" on their base to ease in alignment and to seal the bore. In testing, I have found both of these bullets to be accurate and deadly. My friend Bryan Mason once took a big white-tailed doe at 134 yards using one in a Knight Rifle. The .50 caliber 348-grain bullet was pushed with 100 grains of Pyrodex Select to more than 1,500 fps and penetrated completely, dropping the deer in its tracks.

Another advantage of these bullets is that they load easily. My son, Nathan, could load them when he was six years old, even in a dirty rifle. This aids in accuracy by solving one of the primary problems with conical bullets.

ACCURACY CONSIDERATIONS

Perhaps the biggest problem with conical, full caliber, engraved-on-loading bullets is in achieving consistent accuracy. Flyers are all too common and can be a source of frustration for any shooter. It's not that there is anything wrong with these bullets; it's more in the process of loading them.

There is probably no easy solution to this problem except to use careful attention to loading technique and consistency. Lead is by nature mal-

When using a full caliber conical bullet in a sidelock gun, make sure the rifling twist is fast enough to stabilize the bullet.

Shooting only from a clean bore—that is, cleaning between shots—also ensures that the bullets will pass through the bore easier. It's impossible to control the exact amount of fouling in a dirty bore, so the pressure needed to load the bullet will vary from shot to shot. This inconsistency will also contribute to inaccuracy. If you wish to shoot from a fouled bore, it helps to use a lubricated wad, such as that sold by Ox Yoke Originals, between the bullet and the powder.

BIG BULLETS DO THE JOB

Back when my home state first opened a muzzleloader deer season, my wife gave me a Thompson/Center .54 caliber Renegade rifle for my birthday. First, I put a peep sight on the gun, and then I ordered a bullet mold to cast a 430-grain Thompson/Center Maxi-ball, a conical bullet. With 110 grains of Goex FFg blackpowder, I had 1,470 fps muzzle velocity. It was never the most accurate muzzleloader I have shot, but it wasn't bad either, usually grouping about 2 inches at 50 yards.

For a lot of years, the Renegade was my hunting gun, and every deer it hit made its way to my freezer. I have never recovered a bullet from any animal. Did they expand? Who cares? It's already .54 inch; how big is your .270 after it expands? Doubling its diameter only catches up. I always had easy-to-follow blood trails, and they always led to a dead deer. This early experience convinced me of the reason for the big hole in muzzleloader barrels: Big bullets kill better.

Assuming adequate bore diameter, full caliber lead bullets of any design are one of the best choices a hunter can make. They almost always exit on deer-sized game, leaving behind a long and large wound channel, and they shoot flat enough for any range that a muzzleloader was ever designed for.

leable and will change its shape in response to outside forces. If the bullet is slightly tipped when it's started in the bore, it can enter out of alignment and will not shoot well. Or, if the nose is mashed when engraving the rifling while starting, or if the bullet is jammed down a fouled bore, accuracy will suffer. Bullets can also deform while seating against the powder.

The common loading technique of bouncing the ramrod against a seated bullet is a guessing game that will give you inconsistent seating pressure and almost guarantee nose deformation. Instead, use constant pressure on the rod.

SABOT BULLETS

*T*echnology has mutated the rules, and things have recently changed in the muzzleloader-hunting arena. While they are the most variable in performance and the most controversial, sabot bullets are also likely the most popular with hunters today.

In-line rifles get the blame, but the primary driving force in the current trend to make muzzleloaders emulate modern centerfire rifles is the change to sabot bullets. The in-line design really changed nothing from a technical standpoint, but sabot bullets allowed the hunter access to higher velocities, better accuracy and more complex bullets.

I experimented with sabot bullets quite a bit when they first started to appear on the market. I concluded they were a gimmick and that any hunter who insisted on using them was courting disaster.

Sabot bullets offer a wide range of performance characteristics and are likely the most popular bullets with hunters today.

SABOT STRATEGIES

The manufacturers were attempting to create an illusion of modern rifle performance from a muzzleloader. Because they recognized that most hunters will focus on the wrong things in terms of performance, they correctly saw velocity as the answer.

Hunters will focus on accuracy, but to a greater extent, they will focus on velocity, which in their minds means flatter trajectories. Accuracy and velocity are easy to recognize and to visualize. The concept of terminal performance—neither easily recognizable nor easy to visualize—is often ignored.

For any firearm, but particularly for a muzzleloader, choosing a hunting bullet solely on the basis of its accuracy or its flat trajectory is a big mistake. Terminal ballistics are far more important, but that's what suffered most with the first sabot bullets.

The manufacturers were trying to flatten trajectories by using much smaller and lighter pistol bullets and driving them to higher velocities. They succeeded in both. But they were false gains paid for in the currency of reduced terminal performance.

They were asking pistol bullets to do something they were never intended to do. Back then, these were simple bullets. Most had a thin jacket that was cold-formed over a soft lead core. They were designed to work reasonably well within a small window of impact velocities that were, comparatively speaking, rather low. For example, the mighty .44 Mag. only generated about 1,300 "real world" fps at the muzzle with a 240-grain bullet. Muzzle velocities with the muzzleloaders using this same bullet were approaching 2,000 fps. The bullets couldn't handle it and would come apart on impact, resulting in poor penetration.

A SABOT STORY

I speak from experience on all this. As I type these words, there is a big 9-point set of whitetail antlers hanging over my head. They are all I have from my best blackpowder buck ever. He was hit

These jacketed bullets failed when the jacket separated from the core. This will impede penetration.

with a simple 240-grain .44 pistol bullet at close range and from a sharp downward angle. Impact velocity was more than 2,000 fps but the bullet failed, disintegrating shortly after impact. Of course, there was no exit wound.

The buck dropped in his tracks, but soon got up and ran off. He ran to a small lake surrounded with thick brush, blowdowns and piled driftwood, but with the high entry wound and no exit hole, there was no blood trail. I looked that night until the batteries failed in my flashlight.

After a quick supper, the guys at camp returned with me to find the buck. We even brought a tracking dog, who kept leading us to the same spot on the edge of the lake and stopping. We assumed that with no blood trail, he simply couldn't tell the buck's tracks from all the other deer in the area. We looked until late that night and all the next day but found no sign of the deer.

I know that my companions were doubting my insistence that I had hit the buck. But I had no doubt; it was an easy shot and I know what a hard-hit deer looks like. They don't fall down and roll around on the ground like this one did without a reason. (It was suggested that perhaps he was just laughing at me, but I don't think so.)

I knew what was on everybody else's mind: that I had missed and wouldn't admit that I had. Finally, we gave up.

Several days later, a squirrel hunter smelled

Modern in-line muzzleloaders are designed to work best with sabot bullets.

something bad and followed his nose to the deer. The buck had entered the lake where the dog had kept stopping, and had swum across. It was only 50 yards or so to the other side, but without a boat we couldn't have made the crossing.

We really hadn't thought the deer would have crossed, and though we had scanned the other shore with binoculars, we had concentrated our search on our side of the lake. The buck had been just far enough into the brush that we couldn't see him. He had died in the trail rather than in a bed, which tells me that he was dead within minutes of my shot.

With a better bullet, there would have been an exit hole and a blood trail to follow. There also would have been more penetration so that the deer might not even have made the lake. What I suspect happened was that the bullet only penetrated a few inches, damaging the top of his lungs. It took a while for his lungs to fill with blood, which caused his death.

THINGS GET BETTER

I saw this kind of bullet failure several more times in the following few years. Usually we found the deer, but not always. As a bullet junkie, I make it a practice to check out any critter that's been shot. I spend a lot of time with my head in a deer's chest cavity, digging for bullets and checking wound channels. What I saw again and again with the early sabot bullets only strengthened my resolve not to hunt with them.

Then Randy Brooks brought out his Barnes Expander-MZ muzzleloader bullet. It was based on his hugely successful all-copper X-Bullet for modern rifles.

Here was a solid copper, hollow-point sabot muzzleloader bullet that would fly fast, flat and accurate. The best 100-yard group I have ever fired from a muzzleloader measured .60 inches and it was with the Barnes Expander-MZ bullet.

Sabot bullets allow the hunter to match bullet performance to the game being hunted.

The bullets expanded to astonishing diameters over a wide range of impact velocities, and weight retention was almost always 100 percent. Penetration was mind-boggling when you looked at the huge frontal area.

In the first dozen critters I shot with these bullets, I only recovered two bullets. One hit a whitetail that was facing me, and I found it poking out of the hide on his butt well past a smashed hipbone. The other hit a big Florida hog in the chest. This old warrior had the thickest gristle shield on his chest I have ever seen on a wild hog. The bullet penetrated his mud-encrusted hide, the gristle shield, broke both shoulders and was stuck in the gristle on the off side, just inside the hide. This stuff is so tough that even using a very sharp knife, it still took me fifteen minutes to cut the bullet free.

SABOT ADVANTAGES

My mind was officially changed about sabot bullets in muzzleloaders. I still won't use most pistol bullets. But with the right bullet, a sabot design has a lot of advantages. First and most obvious is that we are no longer exiled to using only soft lead bullets. With sabots, muzzleloaders are now able to use complexly designed expanding bullets. Or we can use solids for deep penetration on really big game.

Instead of a projectile that is bore diameter, sabot style bullets use a much smaller projectile encased in a plastic "sabot" or jacket that is bore diameter. This sabot is designed to pass through the bore like a bullet, filling the grooves and taking on a spin from the rifling. It holds the projectile inside and imparts the spin to the projectile without the bullet ever touching the bore. As it exits the muzzle, the sabot will fly away from the bullet, leaving the projectile to freely travel downrange to the target.

The advantage is that, because it never touches the bore, the projectile can conceivably be made of material that would never work with a conventional bore-sized bullet. A sabot-encased bullet can be made out of lead, steel, titanium or even kryptonite. It does not need to obturate to seal the bore—the sabot takes care of that chore—so soft lead is no longer a requirement.

WORKING GREAT

Now we finally have bullets that work well in a sabot design. In addition to the Barnes bullet, Remington also has an all-copper sabot bullet with similar performance. It's hard to say if the handgun or muzzleloader market drove bullet development, but both have benefited.

Nosler and Winchester teamed up to build a handgun-style Partition bullet. The concept of the Partition is simple. The bullet has two lead cores separated by a wall or "partition" of jacket material. The front core is soft and the jacket is engineered to expand easily. The partition stops the expansion. The harder rear core stays in place and pushes the expanded bullet straight and deep into the target.

This handgun bullet expands reliably and holds together over a wide range of impact velocities. The same bullet that works in the .44 Mag. works

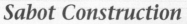

Sabot Construction

Any muzzleloader bullet not used with a sabot must be made only from soft, pure lead. These bullets must obturate and fill the bore; only pure lead will do that correctly. In a sabot, the bullet can be made from just about any material because the sabot fills and seals the bore independent of any bullet obturation.

With sabots, muzzleloaders are now able to use complex design expanding bullets. Left to right: Barnes Expander-MZ, Nosler Partition and Swift A-Frame.

For the Big & Mean Stuff

For the hunter after something larger, tougher or meaner than deer, penetration becomes the prime requisite. C&D Special Products makes a bullet it calls the "Harvester," which is nothing more than a hard-cast, flat-nosed, rifle bullet in a sabot. But handgun hunters have known for generations that this style bullet penetrates deep and is deadly.

Left: C&D Special Products "Harvester." Right: 405 gr. cast bullet from an RCBS mold #45-405-FN.

I have had excellent results using a 405-grain cast bullet from an RCBS mold #45-405-FN designed for the .45-70 Gov. and other similar cartridges. I size it without lube or a gas check to .451 inch in a die designed for the .45 Auto and use a long sabot. This flat-nosed design has long been proven effective on big game. It transfers energy very well, producing good wound channels, and it penetrates straight on large game. Accuracy and velocity are very good and the bullet offers great versatility. I have never recovered one from any critter, including a good black bear that was shot end-for-end.

I usually cast from wheel-weights. This alloy is tough enough to penetrate fully on game as large as elk while still providing a little expansion. For even bigger game, I use the harder linotype so the bullet will act like a solid and penetrate well.

equally well from a muzzleloader. I have shot several deer and hogs with the Partition-HG bullet, both from handguns and muzzleloaders, and it has always performed flawlessly.

Swift's A-Frame is similar to the Partition, but actually takes the design a step further. The front core is bonded to the jacket, so weight retention is even higher. It's available in a wide range of weights.

Remington has incorporated its Core-Lokt design into a jacketed bullet for muzzleloaders. Federal has developed a Trophy Bonded Pistol bullet that it plans to introduce to the muzzleloader market, and Hornady's famous XTP bullet has been toughened in its Mag. Version, to withstand higher impact velocities.

But take care to know which bullet you are buying. The poorly performing bullets are still around and the packaging is not going to say "this bullet

Left is a Nosler Partition and right is a Barnes Expander-MZ. Both recovered from white-tailed deer after traveling end for end.

sucks," so you must know what you are buying.

ACCURACY ADVANTAGES

Another reason for the popularity of sabot bullets is their accuracy. The bullets and sabots are made on precision machinery to very close tolerances, so the potential for accuracy is definitely there.

The sabot starts into the barrel easier than a lead bullet, which means tipped bullets are unheard of. And because most sabot shooters clean between shots, sabots are easier to load and seat. This, combined with tough copper-jacketed bullets, all but eliminates bullet damage during loading.

If tradition doesn't rule you with an iron hand, a good sabot bullet in a design appropriate for the game you are hunting is one of the best choices you can make for muzzleloader big game hunting.

Best Bullet Picks

I don't pretend to have tried every bullet on the market. This would be tough to do with targets, let alone game. Here are my personal picks of some bullets that I have shot and hunted with, along with some other recommendations.

Round Ball Choices

Round balls are not all created alike. Cast bullets have a sprue that must be correctly oriented when loading. Do it wrong and it can affect accuracy. Cast bullets are also subject to voids or air bubbles that can affect accuracy. I don't mean to imply that cast round balls are not good; usually, they are excellent. But my experience is that to achieve this level of quality, I have had to cast my own. Most shooters would rather not bother.

The swaged round balls from Hornady are an excellent alternative. There is no sprue to orient and the quality is always excellent.

Conical Picks

In conical bullets, it's still hard to beat the old standby Thompson/Center Maxi-Ball. I cast my own, but I have shot hundreds of the "store bought" bullets from T/C. If anything, they are better than mine.

Many hunters claim they don't like Maxi-Balls because they don't expand. I can't say for sure if Maxi-Balls expand on game or not because I have never recovered one that hit a deer. But they will expand in testing medium. (Either way, it's the thinking that is flawed. Once again, we are equating muzzleloader performance to modern rifle performance and it's apples to oranges. A muzzleloader bullet of proper design and diameter does not need to expand.)

I have also had good luck with the Hornady Great Plains bullet and Remington's Gamemaster conical. The Black Belt bullet is designed to be slightly under bore diameter so it loads easily, even in a fouled bore. A plastic cup attached to the base guides it and keeps it in place. The bullet obturates on firing and fills the rifling. They are accurate when used correctly.

These are "my picks" for bullets. Front left to right: Hornandy round ball, T/C Maxi-Ball, Hornady Great Plains, Remington Gamemaster, Black Belt. Back left to right: Barnes Expander-MZ .50 300 gr., Barnes Expander-MZ 325-gr. .54, Nosler 250-gr. Partition, RCBS .45-405FN, C&D Harvester, Cabela's X-Tended Range.

Sabot Selections

In sabot bullets, I am very partial to the Barnes Expander-MZ. I have always favored lots of bullet weight, and I like the 300-grain in .50 caliber guns. In .54 caliber guns, I like the 325-grain. For a little more speed and a little less recoil, I have had good luck on whitetails with the Nosler 250-grain Partition bullet.

I like penetration on deer, and demand it on anything larger. Nothing I have tried penetrates and kills better than my own hard-cast, flat-nosed bullets. I cast them from an RCBS .45-405FN mold. I size them to .451 inch and load them with a long sabot. For those who would rather not mess with casting, the C&D Products Harvester bullets are basically the same thing. Other hunters whose opinions I respect tell me they are great.

Cabela's X-Tended Range Sabot uses a pointed, polymer tip bullet. Pointed bullets cut the air better in flight and will retain downrange energy and velocity better. Not only do they deliver more punch at the target, but they have a flatter trajectory as well. I have wondered for years why somebody didn't put a long, pointed bullet in a sabot. Apparently somebody has. If the terminal ballistics are good, this bullet might be a trendsetter in blackpowder hunting bullets.

UNDERSTANDING RIFLING

*J*ust exactly how the concept of rifling in a gun's bore was developed is a bit unclear. It's thought that archers who attached feathers to their arrows noticed that the curved wing feathers caused the arrow to spin in flight and made them more accurate.

Rifling in guns can be traced to the 16th century. Some say it was Gaspard Kollner, a Vienna gun maker, who first put spiral grooves in musket barrels. Others claim that his rifling was straight and that it was Augustus Kotter of Nuremberg who first used spiral rifling in 1520. Another text says that the earliest known rifled gun was a matchlock owned by Emperor Maximillian in 1500.

Regardless of the exact date when rifling was first used to send a bullet spinning in flight, it remained a seldom-used concept for centuries. Rifled barrels were simply too difficult and expensive to make, and only the mega-wealthy could afford such a luxury.

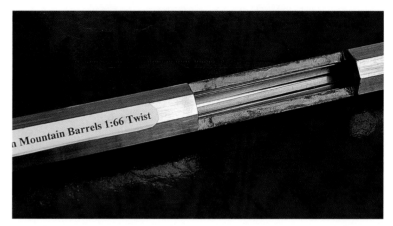

This cut-away of a Green Mountain Muzzleloader barrel shows the rifling.

HOW RIFLING WORKS

Nobody back then knew exactly how rifling worked to make a gun more accurate, but the popular theory was that spinning the bullet kept the Devil from riding it and steering it away from its intended target. Today we know that spinning a bullet stabilizes it with a gyroscopic effect. The gyroscopic effect causes a spinning object to resist a change in direction and that's the real reason the Devil can't steer the spinning bullet away from the target.

This is the same effect that keeps a toy top standing upright while it's spinning. A bullet spinning on its axis will resist outside forces that might cause a non-rotating projectile to veer off course.

Spinning also minimizes the influences of different densities within the bullet (air bubbles, grooves slightly less filled out, and so on) and the differences of slight irregularities on the surface that change air friction. Without the spinning induced by rifling, these slight irregularities would eventually cause the bullet to veer off

course. But with the bullet spinning, those irregularities are in constant motion and so their influence on the bullet's course is minimized. When combined with the much more powerful gyroscopic effect, these two factors create a more accurate projectile.

Rifling is simply a series of parallel "ridges" that spiral within the bore of the rifle barrel. These ridges are called "lands" and the valleys between them are called the "grooves." The distance between the opposing lands is the bore diameter, .50 inch for a .50 caliber muzzleloader. The distance between opposing grooves is the groove diameter, which can vary depending on the depth of the rifling grooves in the barrel. Common rifling depths range from .003 inch with a bore diameter of .506 inch, to .015 inch with a bore diameter of .530 inch.

BULLETS & RIFLING

A conical muzzleloader bullet is designed to take the shape of the lands in its sides while filling the bore to the bottom of the grooves. To accomplish this, the bullet is usually of the same diameter, or slightly larger than the groove diameter. Often there will be a taper that has the base of the bullet at land diameter or smaller to allow the bullet to start into the bore. Then it will taper up to where the front driving band will be groove diameter.

These recovered conical bullets show the marks made by the barrel's rifling.

There are exceptions, such as those bullets that are deliberately made smaller for ease of loading. They are designed to obturate, or swell, when pressure is first applied to the base of the bullet. In doing this, the bullet will expand and fill the bore to the bottom of the grooves.

Because most bullets are the size of the grooves, the lands must etch into the metal. This is a large reason why muzzleloader bullets are made from soft, pure lead. If they were constructed from a hard lead alloy or had a gilding metal jacket like a modern rifle bullet, it would be difficult or impossible to engrave the rifling on the bullet when loading without damaging the bullet. Also, because the bullet is rarely a perfect fit with the bore, even bullets that engrave the rifling on loading must obturate when the gun fires. Only soft, pure lead will do that correctly in a muzzleloader.

With a sabot-encased bullet, the rifling engraves the plastic sabot, which is relatively soft. Because it never physically touches the gun barrel, the bullet can be made from any conceivable material. Sabots allow the use of jacketed, hard-cast or even solid-copper bullets.

With a round ball, the cloth patch acts like a sabot to hold the projectile, mating to the rifling and sealing the bore against propellant gas leakage. But a round ball must obturate to completely seal the bore, so again only pure lead should be used.

RIFLING TWIST RATES

This engraving of the bullet itself or the sabot or patch that cradles it allows the lands to control the bullet and impart a rotational spin as it passes through the bore. The amount of spin is dependent on the rate of twist the rifling has. This twist rate is expressed in the number of inches of forward travel needed to complete one rotation. For example, a bullet traveling down a muzzleloader barrel with a 1:28 twist rate will make one complete rotation in 28 inches of forward movement.

There is a great deal of confusion about which twist rate is best in muzzleloaders. The general rule of thumb is that a bullet that is longer in relation to its diameter will require a faster rate of twist than a shorter bullet. Also, a pointed bullet will need a faster twist than a blunt bullet (because the pointed bullet is longer). Finally, velocity can affect the rate of twist needed to stabilize a bullet. A given bullet will stabilize with a slower twist rate if the velocity is higher; but because muzzleloaders operate within a rather small window of muzzle velocity, this last factor can be ignored when selecting twist rates.

Round balls. Round balls are rather unique in their rifling needs. It's obvious that they will benefit from rifling-imparted spin. But without an elongated body and a defined axis, they have no "front" that needs to remain pointed as the leading edge. A fast twist will tend to intensify any irregularities or imperfections; a slow twist rate has proven to be best.

Also, the round ball has relatively little gripping area where the patch contacts the rifling. This, combined with the higher velocities expected from this lightweight bullet, can cause it to fail when used in a gun with a fast twist rate. The patched round ball simply cannot maintain its grip on the rifling when accelerating rapidly down a barrel with a fast twist. The bullet and/or patch will blow out of its mating with the rifling and will reshape to bore diameter and simply travel down the bore in a straight line. This is known as "stripping" the rifling, and the result is poor accuracy.

While there is no defined twist rate, muzzleloaders designed to shoot round balls commonly

Round balls need a relatively slow rifling twist. This is true with both patched round balls (left) and with the Hornady Hard Balls (right) that use a special plastic sabot rather than a cloth patch.

Finding Your Rifle's Twist Rate

*I*f the twist rate of your gun is not marked on the barrel, it is easy to determine. Here's how. Insert your ramrod with a tight-fitting patch all the way to the bottom of the barrel. Mark a spot on the rod flush with the muzzle and also make another mark that corresponds with the front sight. Slowly pull the rod out, letting it rotate until that mark has made one complete revolution and is again aligned with the front sight. Measure from the other mark on the rod to the muzzle and the distance is your twist rate.

For example, if it took 30 inches of travel for one revolution, the rate is 1:30. For rifles with slow twist rates, you may have to use one-half of a revolution and double the distance. For example, if your rod made one-half a revolution in 33 inches, the twist rate is 1:66.

---

use 1:66. But 1:48 is also very popular, and both shoot round balls quite well. Go figure.

Conical bullets. Different conical bullets require different twist rates. The optimum rate is based on the length of the bullet. While there may be an optimum twist rate for each conical bullet, they will all shoot well over a fairly wide spectrum of rifling twist rates.

It's usually better to select a twist rate that is slightly higher than needed. With all else being equal, an "overstabilized" bullet is more desirable than an "understabilized" bullet. If things are working right, spinning a bullet faster than is necessary to stabilize it will not create any problems. But spinning it too slowly will cause it to become unstable downrange and will usually result in keyholing or the bullet tumbling.

The only problem that comes into play is when the faster spin magnifies imperfections in the bullet—like a tire that's out of balance. This is not a huge problem in modern rifles. But in muzzleloaders, the process of loading from the muzzle with a bullet that engraves the rifling on entry and then must be forced down through an often fouled bore, combined with the use of soft lead in the bullets, can make it easy to induce defects.

Those bullets that are badly deformed on loading will exhibit poor accuracy. In theory, a faster-than-necessary twist rate can amplify this condition. However, in the real world, that bullet will not shoot well regardless of the spin rate, so it's an academic point at best.

Sabot bullets. This bullet-loading issue is the primary reason many hunters get better accuracy from sabot bullets. Sabot bullets are easier to start square with the bore, the plastic takes the rifling easier than lead and, because they are jacketed or

at least made of harder lead, they tend to deform less.

When shooting sabot bullets, you must remember that you are stabilizing a bullet that is smaller than the bore diameter. The twist rate must be predicated on the bullet diameter, not on the sabot diameter. This requires a faster twist rate than with conical bullets, particularly if the weights are similar.

The only way to be sure that your muzzleloader is correctly stabilizing the bullets you wish to hunt with is to shoot them. If they are shooting accurately and punching round holes in the target (as opposed to oblong holes, which can indicate instability), chances are they are well mated to the twist rate of your gun. However, if the accuracy is not what you had hoped for, try a different powder charge before you give up. Sometimes going up or down a little in charge weight will make a big difference in accuracy.

If nothing else, you now have a built-in excuse. If you miss that big buck, it's probably because the twist rate was off a little and the Devil was riding your bullet.

Conical and sabot bullets come in all sorts of shapes, sizes and configurations. Half the fun is finding the one that shoots best!

Recommended Twist Rates for Various Bullets

Below are some recommended rifling twist rates for popular .50 caliber muzzleloader bullets. They were determined using the Barnes Ballistic Program and are based on bullet diameter, length and construction. The program also factors in the material used. For example, the solid-copper bullets made by Barnes have a specific gravity of 8.92 (copper is 8.92 times as dense as water in a given volume) while lead has a specific gravity of 11.33. Jacketed bullets fall somewhere between the two. These are only guidelines, but they will help to illustrate the different rifling twist requirements for various bullets.

Bullet	Style	Weight	Length in Inches	Caliber	Recommended Twist Rate
Round Ball	Patched Round Ball	175 grains	.490	.490	1:72
Big Bore Express Black Belt Bullet	Full Caliber Conical Lead	520 grains	.996	.50	1:36.9
Thompson/Center PTX Power Tip Express	Sabot Jacketed Polymer Tip	250 grains	.778	.45	1:39.2
Remington Gamemaster Solid Point Flat Base	Full Caliber Conical Lead	385 grains	.847	.50	1:43.4
Hornady Great Plains Hollow Base Soft Point	Full Caliber Conical Lead	410 grains	.911	.50	1:40.3
Remington Core-Lokt	Sabot Jacketed Hollow Point	303 grains	.877	.429	1:31.5
Nosler Partition - HG	Sabot Jacketed Hollow Point	250 grains	.797	.429	1:34.6
Barnes Expander-MZ Sabot	Solid Copper Hollow Point	250 grains	.915	.45	1:36.7
Barnes Expander-MZ Sabot	Solid Copper Hollow Point	300 grains	1.056	.450	1:31.8
CVA Power Belt Bullet	Full Caliber Conical Copper Coated Lead	295 grains	.640	.50	1:57.4
Thompson/Center Maxi Hunter	Full Caliber Conical Lead	350 grains	.747	.50	1:49.2
Thompson/Center Maxi-Ball	Full Caliber Conical Lead	320 grains	.758	.50	1:48.5
Thompson/Center Maxi-Ball	Full Caliber Conical Lead	370 grains	.890	.50	1:41.3
RCBS Mold #45-405-FN Sabot	Hard Cast Flat Point	405 grains	1.040	.45	1:28.6
White Systems SuperSlug	Full Caliber Conical Lead	600 grains	1.256	.50	1:29.3

The Velocity Myth

arketers make a science of studying human behavior, and they are, for the most part, very good at what they do. It has not been lost on them that the last couple of generations of hunters have been velocity-oriented.

Since smokeless powder arrived on the scene in 1863, American hunters have experienced a trend to faster and faster velocities. This is fine and even desirable with modern rifles and bullets. Trajectories are flattened, making long-range hits more predictable. Energy rises exponentially with velocity so that any velocity gain brings a much larger gain in energy.

This phenomenon has resulted in big game bullets that are becoming smaller and smaller. At the turn of the last century, a .30 caliber was considered a "small bore" big game rifle cartridge, but today we almost consider them to be "big bores." Today's glory is often in the 7mm, 6.5mm or even .270 bore diameters. It is partly the advancement in bullets that has allowed this switch in direction, but only partly. The bulk of the change is traced directly to smokeless powder and the higher velocities it allows.

While hunters in Gramp's generation were content to smack their whitetails with guns like the .38-55 and velocities that were in the teens (tortoise-slow by today's standards), today's well-equipped hunter is more likely to be shooting a 7mm STW with velocities that exceed 3,200 fps.

Velocity Steered the Market

The marketing folks took notice of this velocity preoccupation, and correctly concluded two things about selling muzzleloaders to the hunting public.

Muzzleloaders are not modern rifles and can never perform the same way that they do. Blackpowder muzzleloading rifles have big holes in their barrels for a reason: It is the source of their power.

First, as previously mentioned, the gun companies realized that if they replicated the look and feel of modern rifles, hunters would buy the concept of blackpowder firearms. Unfortunately, this also creates the perception that these modern muzzleloaders, with their stainless steel and

The trend toward using lighter and faster bullets can get you in trouble with something as tough and ornery as a bear.

synthetic materials, are more advanced and far superior to more traditional blackpowder rifles, and must be unfair to use.

The second strategy the marketing folks grabbed at was to find a way to convince the buying public that, just as it is with our modern rifles, faster is better with muzzleloaders. The ads today hype the speed that the guns are supposed to be able to attain.

What's folly is that the public believes it all. There are two parts to the equation of shooting big game with any gun. First is being able to hit the critter in the right place. Second is being able to deliver a bullet with enough performance to ensure a clean kill under a wide set of circumstances.

Blackpowder limits velocity. A muzzleloader coupled with a heavy bullet will perform better on game than will the same rifle loaded with an ultra-light bullet like the one on the left.

THE VELOCITY ILLUSION

Modern rifles are able to increase power by increasing velocity, but blackpowder (and all its suitable substitutes) is limited in the amount of pressure it can generate, so top velocities are relatively low. Despite some claims to the contrary, it's very difficult to push any hunting bullet much faster than 2,000 fps with blackpowder (or a substitute) in a modern muzzleloader-hunting firearm. In a modern rifle, velocities twice that fast don't generate much excitement anymore.

Like the man said, free lunch is an illusion: To attain the higher velocities, something must be traded. That trade-off is bullet weight and diameter. But muzzleloaders are not modern rifles, and can never perform the same way modern rifles do. Blackpowder muzzleloading rifles have big holes in their barrels for a reason. That's the source of their power.

Energy levels rise exponentially with velocity increases, and any increase in velocity brings a much larger rise in bullet energy. But increasing bullet weight is on a straight-line scale with increasing energy. Double the weight and you double the energy. But double the velocity and you increase the energy fourfold.

For example, with a velocity of 1,500 fps, a 250-grain bullet has 1,249 foot-pounds of energy. If we double the weight to 500 grains, but keep the velocity at 1,500 fps, the energy doubles to 2,499 foot-pounds. However, if we take that same

As much fun as working up a good load is, hunting skills (not long-range shooting) will consistently get you your muzzleloader bucks.

250-grain bullet and double the velocity to 3,000 fps, the energy jumps to 4,997 foot-pounds, or four times as much energy as the same bullet at half the velocity.

How Much Velocity Is Enough?

But with blackpowder muzzleloaders, these dramatic velocity increases are not possible. So more bullet weight is the only answer. Also, it should be recognized that more energy is not necessarily the end-all answer to increasing killing power. A better scale, particularly when dealing with muzzleloaders, is momentum, which gives equal importance to velocity and weight.

With the velocity limitations of blackpowder (and, to a lesser extent, lead bullets), for centuries the only way to increase power has been to drill a bigger hole in the barrel and use a bigger bullet. Bigger bullets make bigger holes in the game, and heavier bullets penetrate better than light bullets. This was particularly true when round balls were the bullet of choice. While conical bullets can be made heavier by making them longer, the only way to increase the weight of a round ball is to make the diameter larger.

A Muzzleloader Kills Differently

Another factor in the velocity equation is in the mechanism that a muzzleloader-hunting rifle uses to kill game.

What kills game with any bullet is tissue damage. Modern high-velocity rifles can rely on expanding bullets and explosive energy transfer. This results in hydrostatic shock—the same thing you witness if you shoot a jug of water with a high-velocity bullet and things explode. When this happens in an animal, the hydraulic action of the rapid energy transfer creates a temporary wound channel that is larger than the one created by the bullet itself. This "stretch" cavity results in tissue damage beyond that caused by the physical contact by the bullet.

Also, with the high-velocity impact of a modern hunting bullet, there are secondary projectiles in the form of bullet or bone fragments that deviate from the bullet's course and cause some secondary tissue damage.

A muzzleloader's much lower impact velocity creates little of this secondary action in and around the wound channel. The light bullets that are being used to create these high muzzle velocities lose that speed very quickly, and the impact velocities are usually much lower than the muzzle velocities that the advertisements tout.

A muzzleloader depends primarily on tissue damage caused by direct contact with the bullet. So the larger the bullet, the deeper it penetrates, the greater the killing power. This is the primary reason we do not hunt deer with .270 caliber muzzleloaders.

Do not succumb to the siren song of the marketing tempters. Ultra-high velocity (by muzzleloader standards) is not the answer for better big game performance. This is particularly true when these velocities are obtained with small diameter, lightweight bullets.

Muzzleloaders are close-range firearms that depend on hunting skills to set up the shot within a reasonable range. Then muzzleloaders depend on bullet weight and diameter to kill game.

That's why they drill those big holes in the barrel.

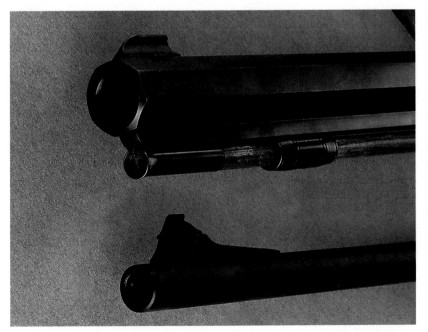

A muzzleloader depends primarily on tissue damage caused by direct contact with the bullet. So the larger the bullet, the deeper it penetrates and the greater the killing power. This is why muzzleloader bores (top) are larger than those on modern rifles.

Chapter 3

MUZZLELOADER PROPELLANTS

From the time Roger Bacon introduced blackpowder to the Western world, until Black Bert discovered that it would propel objects through the air, blackpowder was used mostly for flash and noise.

Once it was discovered how to harness the power of blackpowder and then use it in guns to propel objects with the intent of hitting a distant target, the destiny of modern muzzleloaders was determined.

We used to call muzzleloader hunting "blackpowder" hunting, but with the advent of replica propellants, that term now seems a bit antiquated. But the replicas are designed to mimic blackpowder in burn characteristics and usually in the production of white smoke and in the distinctive sound and smell. The primary purpose of replica propellants is to ease the regulations that are imposed on blackpowder, and make it easier for the average hunter to acquire a propellant needed to fuel his muzzleloader.

It is the propellant that identifies muzzleloader hunting and it's the heart of the concept. Blackpowder has a huge historical significance, and had it never been invented, the world as we know it would be a very different place. Countries and kingdoms were won and lost because of this substance. Men were set free or enslaved with its use. Wilderness was explored and settled. Great nations were built. All because blackpowder existed.

From our perspective today, its primary function is to propel bullets from our hunting guns. There are much better propellants for use in modern guns, but we use blackpowder because without that white smoke, it just wouldn't be muzzleloader hunting. Blackpowder is quaint and antiquated, and we use it to maintain our connection with the past. But we should never lose perspective on the huge historical impact of this substance.

A BRIEF HISTORY OF BLACKPOWDER

Where blackpowder was discovered is not entirely clear. Depending on the historical text you consult, it would appear that the Chinese had some sort of gunpowder as early as the 11th century. The first undisputed record of gunpowder was written in 1248 by a Franciscan Friar named Roger Bacon. He was so spooked by the stuff that he wrote about it in code.

It is said that blackpowder's use for powering projectiles was discovered by the monk of Freiburg, "Black Berthold," or Berthold Schwartz, when he was mixing blackpowder with a mortar and pestle and it ignited, blowing the pestle through the roof. Some say that's only a legend, while others claim that's where the military term "mortar" originated.

Blackpowder remains one of the best propellant choices a muzzleloader hunter can make.

Regardless, it is inarguable that the discovery of this simple substance had a great influence on the course of human history.

Because it ignites at a lower temperature, blackpowder is the best choice for sidelock guns.

Blackpowder is an intimate mechanical mixture of saltpeter (potassium nitrate), charcoal and sulfur.

WHAT IS BLACKPOWDER?

Gunpowder (blackpowder) is an intimate mechanical mixture of saltpeter (potassium nitrate), charcoal and sulfur. Roger Bacon's first recorded formula gives the proportions as 7:5:5. That is 41 percent saltpeter, 29.5 percent charcoal and 29.5 percent sulfur. The proportions gradually changed with the percentage of saltpeter increasing until, by the end of the 18th century, blackpowder reached its final form: 75 percent saltpeter, 15 percent charcoal and 10 percent sulfur.

The earliest powder was called "serpentine" and was a finely ground powder that had some problems. When packed tightly in a gun chamber, it was so fine that it lacked any air spaces. It was difficult to ignite and slow to burn. During storage and transport, it had a tendency to separate into its parts and had to be remixed before use. It was made by grinding the materials separately, combining them and grinding and mixing again. This was dangerous, and any spark could cause an explosion.

During the 15th century, the French invented "corned" powder, in which the three substances were mixed together in the wet state and the resulting paste dried. This was a much safer method than dry mixing, which resulted in short career paths for most practicing the art.

Once dry, the powder was crumbled and passed through sieves to produce granular powder. Such powder was more efficient in the gun, since the interstices (small spaces) between the grains allowed faster ignition and combustion. Also, because each grain was a solid compound, the individual substances could not separate.

It is interesting to note what is said about blackpowder in the Shooter's Bible Small Arms Lexicon and concise Encyclopedia (copyright 1968): "It is a low-order explosive for use in igniters, primers, fuses and blank fire charges. Now almost obsolete."

Obviously, that was written before the muzzleloader hunting boom.

BLACKPOWDER FOR MODERN MUZZLELOADERS

*H*ere is a summary of the different types of blackpowder available to today's muzzleloader hunter.

GOEX

From the 1800s until the start of World War I, there were lots of blackpowder manufacturers in Pennsylvania's upper anthracite region. They existed primarily to fill the blasting needs of the coal mining industry. E. I. Du Pont de Nemours joined the pack, and in 1908 began construction of a plant to make powder in Belin, Pennsylvania. The plant produced its first batches of blackpowder in 1912.

By 1915, the Belin plant had become the second largest producer of blackpowder in the United States. During World War I, World War II and the Korean and Viet Nam conflicts, the Belin plant provided millions of pounds of military blackpowder.

As the direction of military explosives changed,

GOEX is one of the best-known suppliers of blackpowder for today's muzzleloader hunter. It offers in a wide selection of grain sizes to meet just about any muzzleloading requirement.

Blackpowder Ignites Easily

*R*emember that blackpowder ignites at a much lower temperature than most substitutes. This is a big plus with any ignition system, but sidelocks, which require the ignition fire to make a turn to reach the powder, are

Blackpowder has a low ignition temperature and burns very fast.

more prone to misfires or hangfires. I use blackpowder almost exclusively in my sidelock guns. It is also the only choice in a flintlock. Delayed ignition, hangfires or misfires can occur when the ignition is marginal. Because its ignition temperature is lower than substitutes, blackpowder will tilt the odds in your favor a little.

---

demand for blackpowder greatly decreased. In 1973, E. I. Du Pont sold the Belin plant to Gearhart-Owen Industries (GOEX), who retained most of the Du Pont employees.

GOEX moved to the former headquarters of the Louisiana Army Ammunition Plant in Doyline, Louisiana, in late 1997. Currently, GOEX is the sole blackpowder manufacturing facility in North America.

GOEX powder for modern muzzleloaders is offered in the following sizes:

- Cartridge
- Fg
- FFg
- FFFg
- FFFFg

Elephant brand blackpowder is imported from Brazil by Petro-Explo, Inc. of Arlington, Texas. It provides a lower cost powder that gives good performance.

Elephant Black Powder

Elephant Black Powder is made in Brazil and imported by Petro-Explo, Inc., in Arlington, Texas. The Pernambuco Powder Company has been making Elephant Black Powder since 1866, but it's only been imported and available for modern muzzleloader shooters since 1992. Elephant manufactures its own charcoal and uses only wood from the umbauba tree, which has been found to provide the quality of charcoal Elephant demands.

One attractive feature of Elephant Black Powder is its low retail price.

Elephant's Sporting Powder is offered in the following grades:

Cannon Grade *2.0 mm to 1.9 mm.* This is used primarily in cannons.

Fg *1.68 mm to 1.19 mm.* Recommended for small cannons or large muskets.

FFg *1.19 mm to .59 mm.* Recommended for large-bore rifles and handguns .45 caliber and larger. Also muskets and blackpowder cartridge guns.

FFFg *.84 mm to .30 mm.* Recommended for use in small-caliber rifles and handguns. Also blackpowder cartridges.

FFFFg *.42 mm to .15 mm.* Used as a priming powder for flintlock muzzleloaders.

Swiss Black Powder

Since 1999, Petro-Explo, Inc., has also imported Swiss Black Powder, which, as you might have guessed, is made in Switzerland. The Blackpowdermill Aubonne was founded in 1853. James Kirkland, Vice President of Petro-Explo, says that the same attention to detail and precision that made the Swiss famous for watches and pocket knives is applied to making this powder. The result, he says, is the finest powder made. The price reflects the quality of this powder.

Petro-Explo makes its charcoal from the old standby buckthorn alder, which has been a favorite with European powder makers for centuries. According to Kirkland, the Swiss powder is so powerful and efficient that all loads should be cut by 20 percent to achieve the same pressure and velocity as other blackpowders.

The Swiss powder size rating system is a little different from what we are used to here in the States, but it's easily converted to our more familiar rating system. Swiss powder is available in:

Swiss No. 1 = FFFFg *.5 mm to .2 mm.* Used as a priming powder for flintlock muzzleloaders.

Swiss No. 2 = FFFg *.87 mm to .5 mm.* Recommended for use in small-caliber rifles and handguns under .45 caliber.

Swiss Black Powder is imported by Petro-Explo. It is a very high-grade powder and will produce higher velocities with a given charge weight than other blackpowders.

WANO Blackpowder is manufactured by WANO Schwarzpulver GmbH of Liebenburg, Germany and is imported by Luna Tech, Inc., Owens Cross Roads, Alabama.

Swiss No. 3 = FFg *1.36 mm to .7 mm.* Recommended for large-bore rifles and handguns .45 caliber and larger. Also blackpowder cartridge guns.

Swiss No. 4 = 1-1/2 Fg Schuetzen Powder *1.36 mm to .9 mm.* Used in blackpowder cartridge rifles and muskets.

Swiss No. 5 = Fg *1.6 mm to 1.2 mm.* For use in large-caliber blackpowder cartridge rifles.

WANO

WANO Blackpowder is manufactured by Wano Schwarzpulver GmbH of Liebenburg, Germany, and is imported into NAFTA countries by Luna Tech, Inc., of Owens Cross Roads, Alabama.

WANO is available in four grades that are consistent with the grades and applications of other blackpowders.

• Fg
• FFg
• FFFg
• FFFFg

WANO also offers unglazed powder in three grades that may have some application to the blackpowder hunter:

• FFa (Slightly larger than Fg, suitable for cannon.)

• FFFFa (Between Fg and FFg.)

• FFFFFFFa (Less fine than FFFFg, and may be used for priming, because unglazed powder ignites easier than glazed.)

DISPENSING BLACKPOWDER

Blackpowder is unstable, unpredictable and easy to set off. It can be ignited by heat, friction, compression, impact or crushing. Any spark, even from static electricity, can cause it to ignite, and trust me—you don't want to be there when it does.

I have seen the results of a large quantity of blackpowder that has ignited unexpectedly, and it ain't pretty. I am not talking about an explosion. For that, the powder needs to be contained. Rather, I am talking about powder that accidentally ignited in an opened-top bucket, sending two old friends to the hospital for long and very painful stays. The scars are disfiguring and permanent, but my friends are alive. They came very close to experiencing a more final and permanent result.

If you do a lot of shooting, it's always easier to dispense several premeasured loads into speed loaders or other holders. Obviously, a bench-mounted powder measure will make this chore much easier.

The Hornady Static-Resistant Blackpowder Measure is designed to be safe with blackpowder.

Although the temptation is great, you should never use the smokeless-powder measure on your reloading bench to dispense blackpowder. Being ignorant of the danger, I have done this in the past. When I learned of the maiming, death and loss of property associated with the practice, I stopped. I also lay awake at night, my stomach hurting from the knowledge that I dodged a very big bullet. I could have been killed or at least burned to charcoal. I could have burned my house down and endangered my wife and kids, all because I didn't know any better.

I know of a guy in a nearby town who wasn't so lucky. Nobody knows for sure what happened because he and his building were mixed in the same smoldering pile of ashes, but the prevailing theory is that he was using blackpowder in a powder measure that was designed for smokeless powder.

Pre-measure your powder charges under safe, controlled conditions and you can load up confidently at the range or in the field.

The plastic in the reservoirs used on most powder measures can store or create static electricity, and the metal rotating or sliding drums can cause a spark. Also, the drum is designed to cut any smokeless powder kernels that are caught in it, but this can cause an impact ignition of blackpowder.

If you plan to use a powder measure, make certain it is one designed for blackpowder use. For example, the Hornady Static-Resistant Blackpowder Measure is designed for muzzleloader use. It features an aluminum (rather than plastic) hopper and cap. The metering system is brass to prevent the possibility of sparks. It's calibrated in 5-grain increments to 50 grains and then 10-grain increments to 130 grains. With this device and a handful of homemade holders, I can safely dispense enough premeasured powder charges for a day's shooting in just a few minutes.

Blackpowder Square Mesh Screen Sizes

(in inches)

	GO	NO-GO
Fg	.0689	.0582
FFg	.0582	.0376
FFg	.0376	.0170
FFFg	.0170	.0111

PYRODEX: THE "MODERN" BLACKPOWDER

For centuries the only powder available for use in firearms was blackpowder. That lock on the market continued until 1863, when smokeless powder hit the shooting scene. Soon blackpowder was all but forgotten, at least for hunting firearms.

Then along came the muzzleloader boom of the 1970s, and suddenly blackpowder was back in vogue.

But things had changed since 1863. Blackpowder had become classified as a "Class A Explosive," which severely restricted its shipment, sale and storage. There were always rumors of a replacement that would be classified, like smokeless powder, as a "Flammable Solid," allowing easier and less costly shipping and less restrictive sales and storage requirements.

Pyrodex was the first modern blackpowder substitute.

THE BIRTH OF PYRODEX

The market remained void of a viable alternative to blackpowder until R. E. Hodgdon first met with Dan Pawlak in January 1975 at Mr. Pawlak's home in Issaquah, Washington. Hodgdon was surprised to find that Pawlak had a complete laboratory next to his home. It featured transducer pressure guns, oscilloscopes, chronographs, lab equipment and an assortment of chemicals.

Pawlak demonstrated his invention for Hodgdon, showing first what happened with blackpowder. With that old standby, the time-pressure curves would rise with each successive shot, demonstrating the effects of powder fouling left in the barrel.

Then they repeated the test with a product called "Pyrodex," a term that Pawlak came up with by shortening "pyrotechnic deflagrating explosive." The time-pressure curves were pretty much the same as those seen in the second shot with blackpowder. The difference was that they remained constant with successive shots. One could be superimposed over the other with no clear difference. Clearly, this propellant produced much less barrel fouling and had little or no accumulative effect relating to pressure.

It became listed as a Flammable Solid and so could be handled and sold like smokeless powder.

Today, this means your local sporting goods store can sell it without special licenses, restrictions or complicated and expensive storage facilities.

Hodgdon and Pawlak were soon in business together and by April 1977, they were shipping the first cans of Pyrodex. Then tragedy struck, and an accident destroyed the plant, killing Pawlak and three other employees. The technical term is that a "deflagration" occurred. (Deflagration is an explosion during which power builds up smoothly and evenly. This contrasts with "detonation," when the explosion is sudden, violent and practically instantaneous.) Regardless of the specifics of the physics involved, the results were devastating on both a personal and business level for all involved.

Hodgdon ultimately decided to continue; he built a plant in Kansas that began shipping Pyrodex again by mid-1979.

Using Pyrodex by Weight

Pyrodex is designed to be comparable with blackpowder by volume and not weight. That is, a powder measure that holds 100 grains of blackpowder will hold the equivalent of 100 grains of blackpowder in Pyrodex, but the actual weight of the Pyrodex will be something different. Any loads using Pyrodex should always be prepared with a volume measure and never a weight scale.

Historically, blackpowder has been loaded on a volumetric basis, even in cartridges. Pyrodex is designed to be a volume-to-volume replacement for blackpowder and is specifically formulated to be used with volumetric measures designed for blackpowder.

But if you feel like you must measure Pyrodex by weight, the manufacturer suggests that you follow these steps. To complete the loading process, you must have:

1. Volumetric blackpowder measure (do not use a measure designed for smokeless powders).

2. Powder scale.

3. Calculator. Because each lot of Pyrodex is regulated by volume, the actual weight of the powder may vary from lot to lot.

For each new lot number you will:

1. Fill the blackpowder volumetric measure to the desired level.

2. Pour the contents into the scale's weighing pan and record the weight. Repeat nine times.

3. Average the weight of the 10 charges. This weight will be the correct charge weight

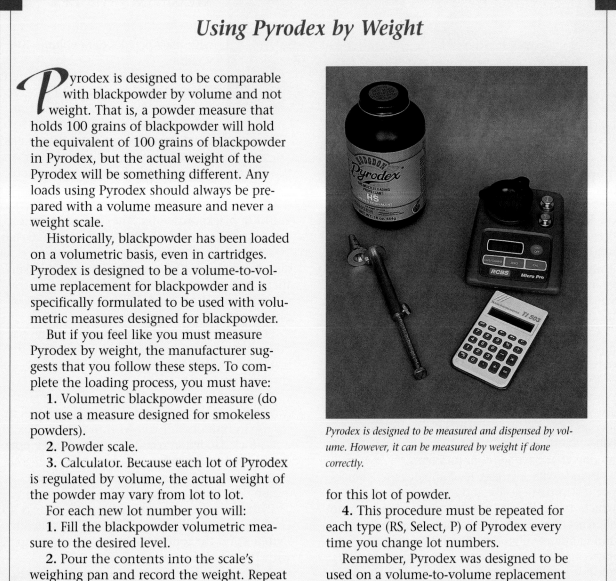

Pyrodex is designed to be measured and dispensed by volume. However, it can be measured by weight if done correctly.

for this lot of powder.

4. This procedure must be repeated for each type (RS, Select, P) of Pyrodex every time you change lot numbers.

Remember, Pyrodex was designed to be used on a volume-to-volume replacement basis with blackpowder. Increased accuracy is usually not achieved by the practice of weighing each charge.

Pyrodex is available in powder form (right) or as pellets (left).

TYPES OF PYRODEX

Now, more than 20 years later, Pyrodex remains the leader in blackpowder substitutes. As ever, there are challengers to its dominance in the field, but Pyrodex has never seriously been in danger of losing the top slot. Where the new substitutes will be in another 20 years remains to be seen, but the safe bet is that they will still be chasing Pyrodex for that coveted lead.

Currently, Pyrodex is offered in three grades of powder as well as in solid "pellet" form. The powders are:

Pyrodex P. Pyrodex P compares to 3F blackpowder in particle size and in usage. It's best in any caliber pistol and in smaller-bore rifles .45 caliber and smaller, particularly when using round balls. Pyrodex P is also useful as a priming charge in guns that have ignition problems.

Pyrodex RS. Pyrodex RS compares to 2F blackpowder in particle size and in use designation, which means it's well-suited for use in most, if not all, current modern muzzleloader hunting rifles and handguns. Pyrodex RS can be used in all calibers of percussion muzzleloading rifles and shotguns. It has a wide variety of uses and is the most versatile powder in the Pyrodex line. Like all grades of Pyrodex, it burns cleaner and produces less fouling than blackpowder.

Pyrodex Select. Select is an enhancement to the RS grade of Pyrodex. It is, in effect, the most carefully produced in a given lot, with extra atten-

tion paid to grain size. Using RS or 2F blackpowder data in a volumetric measure, Select can significantly reduce group size. What is wonderful news to the deer hunter is that Select performs well with sabots and conical bullets. Select has also become a favorite among many blackpowder cartridge shooters because of its exceptional consistency. For target use it is the "best of the best."

MEASURING PYRODEX

Pyrodex is designed to be used with blackpowder data volume-to-volume.

Although weights will be different between blackpowder and Pyrodex, the charge should be based on the weight setting for blackpowder. For example, if you are using 100 grains of blackpowder, you would keep your powder measure at exactly the same setting and use that setting for the amount of Pyrodex that will produce the same ballistic result as the 100 grains of blackpowder did. They fill exactly the same space, but while the blackpowder will weigh 100 grains, the same amount of Pyrodex will actually weigh about 30 percent less. This also means that a one-pound can of Pyrodex will allow 30 percent more shots than the same weight can of blackpowder.

Never measure Pyrodex by weight. Always use a volumetric powder measure that is calibrated for blackpowder, and dispense your charges based on the volume.

Pyrodex is recommended for percussion and cartridge firearms only and is not recommended for use in flintlocks. If you wish to use Pyrodex in a flintlock, Hodgdon recommends that FFFg powder be used in the priming pan and that a 5 grain priming load of FFFg be poured into the barrel before the Pyrodex is added.

Pyrodex produces less barrel fouling and, as it is used repeatedly, the barrel becomes "seasoned" to Pyrodex and the fouling is decreased. Clean up with Pyrodex is basically the same as with blackpowder, and it is recommended that firearms be cleaned immediately after use.

PYRODEX PELLETS

*I*n the early 1980s, The Pyrodex Corporation was involved in research for mortar round igniters, and the research-and-development crew discovered some interesting characteristics in a pressed cake of Pyrodex used for this purpose.

During a brainstorming session it was suggested that pressed cakes, or pellets, of Pyrodex could also be used as muzzleloader charges. Dean Barrett, chief of manufacturing, started research in the late 1980s. Although the pellets showed promise, they had some ignition problems, and the project was shelved.

When in-line muzzleloaders came along, everything changed. Their more positive, straight-line ignition system made the pellets viable. As the market expanded and it became clear that in-lines would dominate the hunting world, Barrett decided to take another look at the pellets. By 1996, it had become apparent that he was on to something, and he applied for a patent.

TAKING OVER

Original production projections thought that one large hydraulic press would fill demand. One year later, three machines couldn't keep up. By

Pyrodex pellets are the choice for many of today's hunters.

1997, Pyrodex pellets had the market standing on its ear, and Pyrodex has never looked back.

I have a confession to make. Ever since Hodgdon came out with the Pyrodex pellet in 1996, I have rarely used anything else for propellant when I am hunting with an in-line muzzleloader rifle. The pellets are so fast and easy to use in the field that I doubt I'll be changing my preference any time soon.

Pyrodex pellets are a solid form of Pyrodex in a premeasured weight equivalent. The pellet is cylindrical, with a hole through the center to aid in burning. One end has a secret-formula black ignition cap (actually, it's blackpowder) that aids in lighting the pellet.

The most popular size is the 50-grain, .50 caliber pellet. It averages about .455 inches in diameter and is about .720 inches long. The hole through the center is .125 inches (⅛ inch). The .50 caliber 50-grain pellet actually weighs about 37.5 grains, but it is the equivalent of 50 grains of FFg blackpowder. Pellets are also available in 30-grain .50 caliber and in 60-grain .54 caliber. There are also .44/.45 caliber 30-grain pellets designed for use in cap-and-ball revolvers.

Hodgdon recommends Pyrodex pellets be used only in in-line rifles. He does not

Hunters like the speed and convenience of using Pyrodex pellets.

recommend they be used in sidelocks or flintlocks. (Although Thompson/Center Arms now has both sidelock and flintlock rifles called "Firestorm" that are designed to be used with Pyrodex pellets.)

Hodgdon also recommends that the pellets never be used in any combination that equals more than 100 grains. Many companies are making guns that they advertise as "3-pellet" rifles, but the company that makes the pellets does not condone those 150-grain loads.

SHOOTING WITH PELLETS

Pyrodex pellets are designed to be used with sabot bullets. They are not recommended for use with conical bullets or round balls unless a fiber or felt wad is used behind the bullet. Conical bullets should only be used with charges of 100 grains for .50 caliber. Hodgdon does not recommend conical bullets and Pyrodex pellets in any .54 caliber muzzleloader.

Hodgdon also recommends that, when shooting a .50 caliber rifle, you should use sabots designed for use with .45 caliber bullets. Sabots designed for .44 caliber bullets are not proven to work as well. When shooting a .54 caliber rifle, Hodgdon suggests that you use sabots designed for use with .50 caliber bullets. The bullet may be either a .50 caliber handgun bullet or a .50 caliber conical bullet. Both will fit the sabot and produce good accuracy. Those .54 caliber rifles using sabots designed for .44 or .45 caliber bullets have proven to be inaccurate.

"Proper sabot selection is critical for good performance," the Pyrodex loading manual says. "If the shooter has a problem with the sabot, it will be immediately apparent. When a sabot fails, it is a catastrophic failure causing very large groups, not a simple opening of the group. If the shooter has a question about sabot performance, it is not difficult to find fired sabots for examination. Failed sabots will be blown to pieces while a sabot that performs well will always have an intact base even though it may lose a petal or two."

The manual also notes that "late in the testing and evaluation of .54 caliber sabots, C&D Special Products, Inc., developed a 54/45 sabot that is successful with .54 caliber Pyrodex pellets. For additional information on this sabot and how to identify it, contact C&D Special Products, 1-800-922-6287."

Hodgdon says to always use one-piece sabots with Pyrodex pellets. Multi-piece sabots do not stand up to pellets very well.

The manual also instructs, "Before shooting Pyrodex pellets, the nipple and breech plug must be clean and dry for proper ignition to occur. This is true of loose powder as well as Pyrodex pellets. To guarantee a clean and dry nipple and breech plug, the nipple should be cleaned with a pipe cleaner followed by a nipple pick used to clean out the flash hole. The same treatment should be given to the breech plug. After careful cleaning, spray a commercially available gun degreaser through the nipple and the breech plug. These high-pressure degreasing sprays will flush all solid debris, lubricants, solvents and moisture from the flash channel providing an uninhibited path for the flash to follow from nipple to pellet."

The only downside of pellets, other than the slightly higher cost, is that you get a fixed product. The pellets are not designed to be modified in any way, so you are restricted to equivalent charge weights that can only be created from multiples of the weights offered. But it's a rare gun that won't shoot well with some combination of pellets.

The Thompson/Center Arms Firestorm flintlock is unique because it is designed to work with powder or Pyrodex pellets.

When loading with Pyrodex pellets, always seat the bullet firmly on top of the pellets, but not so hard that you crush them.

LOADING & OPTIONS

When loading pellets, always seat the bullet firmly on top of the pellets, but not hard enough to crush them. This technique is a little different from the powder packing pressures that most of us have used for years. It takes a little practice to find the line between seating the bullet with enough pressure and crushing the pellets. It's easy enough to develop the skill and once you figure it out, loading with Pyrodex pellets couldn't be simpler or faster. By the way, crushed pellets will fire, but rarely are accurate.

Pyrodex pellets are available in the following configurations.

.50 Caliber, 50-Grain Pyrodex pellets. This is the original Pyrodex pellet, the one that started a muzzleloader hunting revolution. They are designed for use in .50 caliber, in-line rifles. Hodgdon says that a single 50/50 pellet may be used for a light target or small game load, but they are a bit expensive for target shooting; I'll stick with powder for that. But for hunting, the pellets shine. I usually use two 50/50 pellets with a sabot bullet appropriate to the game I am hunting.

.50 Caliber, 30-Grain Pyrodex pellets. Designed as a companion to the original 50/50 Pyrodex pellet, the 50/30 pellet allows each shooter to tailor loads for a specific rifle, projectile and use. The 50/30 pellets may be used in any combination, with other 50/30 pellets or with 50/50 pellets in charges up to a maximum load of 100 grains equivalent.

I tried these for my kids, who were young and a bit sensitive to recoil. I loaded their muzzleloaders with Nosler 250-grain Partition bullets and one 50-grain pellet under a 30-grain pellet. The guns shot well and the velocity was fine for whitetail hunting. Then one day I forgot the 30-grain pellets and loaded their guns with two 50-grain pellets, the same load I was using. Neither kid noticed the difference in recoil. The chronograph showed more velocity, and it was simpler for me.

44/45 Pyrodex pistol pellets. These 30-grain volume-equivalent pellets are designed for use in .44 or .45 caliber cap-and-ball revolvers.

.54 caliber, 60-grain Pyrodex pellets. If, like me, you like the brute power of a .54 caliber rifle and the convenience of Pyrodex pellets, then you will love this pellet.

The convenience of Pyrodex pellets is available for the powerful .54 caliber in-line rife. When coupled with a .54 caliber sabot using a .50 caliber bullet (or selected .45 caliber bullet), Pyrodex .54 caliber/60-grain equivalent pellets offer an accurate, powerful and easy load for a big-bore rifle.

OTHER PROPELLANTS

As with any attractive market, manufacturers keep finding other options. Here are some alternative propellants that are available for muzzleloader hunters.

GOEX CLEAR SHOT: A BLACKPOWDER SUBSTITUTE

GOEX offers a sugar-based muzzleloading blackpowder replica propellant powder called Clear Shot. It's a ball powder that's available in FFg and FFFg sizes.

Clear Shot is meant to be a volume-for-volume substitute for blackpowder. However, it is very close in weight as well. Using the Helium Pycnometer method to measure specific gravity, GOEX found that blackpowder has a specific gravity of 1.92 to 2.08, while Clear Shot's specific gravity is 1.8 to 1.95. Clearly, they are in the same range in terms of weight-to-volume ratio. However, like all muzzleloader propellants, Clear Shot is designed to be measured by volume.

According to GOEX, Clear Shot has been designed to perform exactly like blackpowder and is an excellent replacement for any other replica blackpowder propellants. Clear Shot is a new concept in propellants and it does not contain ascorbic acids or perchlorates. The powder is clean-burning, producing very little residue, so fouling does not build up from shot to shot.

Clear Shot is noncorrosive. It contains nothing that will corrode a gun barrel. It's nonhygroscopic—that is, it does not pick up moisture, even in very high humidity.

Clear Shot has an indefinite shelf life and does not deteriorate or become unstable over time. It produces consistent velocities and low standard deviations. It generates pressures no greater than other replica blackpowder propellants or blackpowder. Reference data provided by GOEX shows that Clear Shot produced velocities and pressures similar to blackpowder. This testing was conducted with rifle cartridges, but muzzleloader

GOEX's sugar-based blackpowder substitute is called Clear Shot.

pressures should follow the same line in terms of pressure.

Other data provided by GOEX was gathered with a Parker Hale Whitworth muzzleloader rifle with a 35-inch .451 barrel with a hexagonal bore and a 1:20 twist. The testers used a 475 grain .451 cylindrical, flat-base, 6-lube groove cast bullet from Navy Arms (lubricated with SPG lube), with shooting conditions at 60°F with a relative humidly of 20 percent and an elevation of 3,000 feet above sea level. A Dynamit Nobel #1081 Wing Musket Cap was used. Charges were weighed at 65 grains. Five shots with GOEX FFg blackpowder provided an average velocity of 1,150 fps, plus or minus 11 fps. Five shots with GOEX Clear Shot FFg had an average velocity of 1,154 fps, plus or minus 11 fps. I would say that performance is about as close as you can get to being the same, at least in terms of velocity and deviation.

Clear Shot has a 1.3C (Class B) DOT Shipping Status, meaning it can be shipped and stored just like smokeless powder.

Finally, clean up is easy and requires only water.

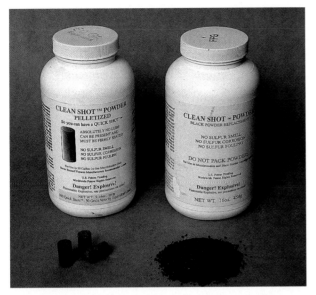

Clean Shot Powder is available in pellet and powder form.

CLEAN SHOT POWDER

One of the new blackpowder substitutes to hit the market is Clean Shot powder. This is a citrus-based powder designed to be used volume-to-volume as a substitute for blackpowder. Clean Shot is available in FFg and FFFg as well as pellets in .50 caliber, 50-grain and .44 caliber, 30-grain equivalent.

According to Clean Shot Technologies (CST), Clean Shot powder is best described as replica blackpowder. It does not contain nitro-cellulose, and it is not a smokeless propellant. It is a propellant designed for use in percussion and blackpowder cartridge arms. Clean Shot powder is not blackpowder, but it does smoke. It is classified by the Department of Transportation as a flammable solid in limited quantities and can be shipped by most common carriers.

Clean Shot powder is intended to be used on a volume-to-volume basis with blackpowder and will give approximately the same velocity and pressure as blackpowder.

Clean Shot powder does not contain sulfur, so there will be no sulfur fouling, sulfur odor or sulfur-related corrosion when using it. CST says it is not necessary to clean the bore between shots, but that the gun should always be cleaned after the shooting session. Clean Shot powder is recommended for use in all modern muzzleloaders, including flintlocks.

Eugene Davenport is the primary distributor for Clean Shot and might be its biggest fan. His favorite load is 90 grains of Clean Shot powder behind a 348-grain Black Belt conical bullet. He uses this in his Thompson/Center Encore 209X50 muzzleloader for a muzzle velocity of 1,535 fps. "This load cuts bullet holes at 50 yards," he told me. "It's devastating on whitetails."

Clean Shot Powder: Load/Velocity Chart

Data provided by Clean Shot Technologies

STANDARD LOADS

Rifle Caliber	Bullet Weight (grains)	Powder Charge (grains by volume)	Velocity (fps)
45	240	60	1,583
50	410	90	1,574
58	510	60	1,123

HIGH-PERFORMANCE LOADS

Rifle Caliber	Bullet Weight (grains)	Powder Charge (grains by volume)	Velocity (fps)
45	250	100	1,880
45	340	100	1,662
50	200	100	1,783
50	410	90	1,574

Davenport has a little advice when using the pellet form of Clean Shot. "Start with a completely clean and dry barrel. Make sure all solvent, oil or water is removed and that you pop a couple of caps to clean the fire channel. Because my gun shoots from a fouled bore to a different point of impact than it does from a clean bore, I pour some powder down the barrel and fire it into the air. This completely dries all the water or solvent and pre-fouls the bore. With Black Belt bullets, you can keep shooting without cleaning as long as you use Clean Shot.

"Always mark your ramrod on the first load to measure how far it will go into the barrel with a proper bullet and charge loaded correctly. With subsequent shots, make sure the bullet is seated against the powder and that the ramrod is down to the line. The air space around the powder pellets causes a small ring of fouling in the bore that causes the next bullet to hang up about a quarter inch from being seated. Make sure you push the bullet firmly against the powder and past this fouling. This provides the best performance and accuracy."

QUICK SHOT PELLETS

Clean Shot powder is also offered in a pellet form called Quick Shot. Quick Shot pellets are pre-measured 50-grain and 30-grain equivalent charges of Clean Shot powder. The .50-grain pellet is for use in modern rifles and pistols .50 caliber and larger. The 30-grain pellet is for .44 caliber

Pellets or powder, Clean Shot works equally well in either form.

Quick Shot Pellets: Load/Velocity Chart
Data provided by Clean Shot Technologies

Rifle Caliber	Bullet Weight (grains)	Quick Shots™	Velocity (fps)
.50	180-grain lead, .45 caliber sabots	30-grain equivalent	867
.50	180-grain lead, .45 caliber sabots	50-grain equivalent	1,438
.50	180-grain lead, .45 caliber sabots	30 grain + 30 grain	1,747
.50	180-grain lead, .45 caliber sabots	30 grain + 50 grain	1,819
.50	180-grain lead, .45 caliber sabots	30 grain + 30 grain + 50 grain	2,058
.50	180-grain lead, .45 caliber sabots	50 grain + 50 grain	2,213
.50	180-grain lead, .45 caliber sabots	30 grain + 30 grain + 30 grain + 30 grain	2,361
.50	180-grain lead, .45 caliber sabots	30 grain + 50 grain + 50 grain	2,406
.50	200 grains	50 grain + 50 grain	1,750
.50	356 grains	50 grain + 50 grain	1,619
.50	356 grains	50 grain + 50 grain + 50 grain	1,986

Note 1: Do not use lubes, lubed patches or oils with any Clean Shot products. No need for cleaners or solvents between shots.

Note 2: Quick Shot pellets produce comparable velocities to Clean Shot powder, blackpowder, Pyrodex pellets or Pyrodex when using the same rifle, bullet and powder charge.

Should you use blackpowder or a substitute?

and larger. Quick Shot pellets are made entirely of Clean Shot powder. Each container of Quick Shot contains 100 pellets.

The company recommends the projectile be seated firmly on the Quick Shot pellets. Even if the Quick Shot should get crushed in loading, they say that nothing is lost in velocity and accuracy.

Any combination of 50-grain or 30-grain equivalent charges can be used to obtain the charge you wish to shoot.

WHICH POWDER IS RIGHT?

Here are some guidelines and ideas on which powder(s) or substitute(s) may be right for you, your gun and your hunting situation.

BLACKPOWDER

Which powder to use? Well, you can never go wrong with blackpowder. The best accuracy in many of the guns that I have tested, including all popular designs, is often found with blackpowder.

Because it ignites easily and hang-fires are almost unheard of, I hunt almost exclusively with blackpowder when I am using sidelock guns. The ignition is not as powerful in a sidelock as it is in an in-line, and the lower ignition temperature of blackpowder provides a margin of safety to ensure that the gun will go off when it's important.

I am not experienced enough with some of the newer blackpowder substitutes to comment on their reliability in a sidelock gun, but at least one

Today's muzzleloader hunter has more propellant options than at any time in history.

manufacturer claims ignition temperatures in the same range as blackpowder. However, there is more than just ignition temperature to consider. Blackpowder has irregular-shaped grains with lots of sharp edges. Just as split-kindling wood is easier to light with a match than chunk firewood, these sharp edges provide an easy place for the powder to start burning.

The downside for blackpowder is availability. Blackpowder falls under some special restrictions (it may get a lot worse if the anti-gun crowd gets its way), and not every gun store can sell it.

Blackpowder also tends to foul more than other propellants. This is not a big factor if you are shooting sabot bullets, as you should clean the bore between shots anyway. Loading a second shot in a fast-breaking hunting situation is not a problem, but the fourth or fifth shot might be. With conical bullets, if the bore becomes fouled, it may make loading the bullet hard, causing a deformed bullet and leading to poor accuracy. But if you clean often and/or use the proper bullet lubricants, blackpowder fouling is not a big problem, particularly in hunting situations.

Blackpowder is graded by kernel size, which determines burning rate. Most big game muzzleloaders will use FFg. FFFg is finer grained and faster burning and is used mostly for small-bore rifles and in handguns. FFFFg is used for priming flintlocks, and Fg is used mostly in cannons or extremely big-bore rifles and shotguns.

Finally, consider that it all started with blackpowder. By using blackpowder, you historically are connected to muzzleloader hunting in a way that no modern substitute can provide. The smoke, smell and sound from the firing of a blackpowder-charged muzzleloader is sure to stir something deep in the soul of any muzzleloader addict.

BLACKPOWDER SUBSTITUTES

Hodgden Pyrodex was the first successful blackpowder substitute and is still by far the most popular and best-known. Pyrodex can be shipped, stored and handled like smokeless powder, eliminating many of the availability problems associated with blackpowder. Although it's a bit more expensive, Pyrodex is far easier to find in most locations. Because it is loaded by volume and weighs less than blackpowder, each pound provides about 30 percent more shots than blackpowder, so the cost starts to balance out.

Pyrodex also burns cleaner than blackpowder and creates less bore fouling. But it is harder to ignite because of a much higher ignition temperature, and is more prone to hang-fires or misfires than blackpowder. In a hunting situation, this can sometimes lead to problems, particularly when the ignition system is borderline to start with. This is particularly true with some of the imported, less expensive sidelock guns.

While they're fine guns for the money, manufacturers have to make some allowances to keep the costs down on the rifle. Those shortcomings are usually found in the final polish of the parts. Often the ignition channels are not as smooth or well-finished as they are with more expensive guns, and this small factor can affect the intensity of the ignition fire that reaches the powder charge. With Pyrodex and likely some other substitutes, this can lead to hang-fires and misfires under certain

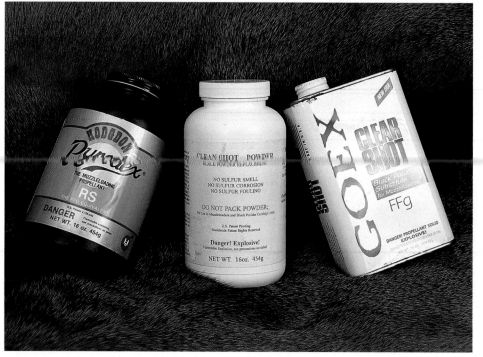

The three most popular blackpowder substitute propellants.

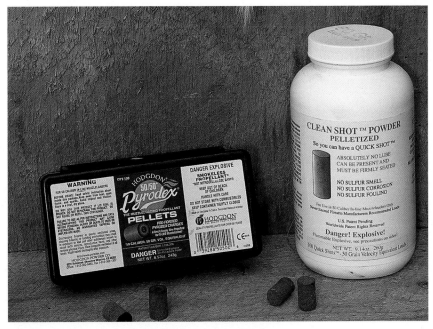

Both Pyrodex and Clean Shot offer pre-formed pellets.

ferent. Always select your loads by volume, not by weight, with any of the current blackpowder substitutes.

CLEAN SHOT & CLEAR SHOT

The other two current substitutes are Clean Shot and Clear Shot. They are graded in Fg equivalents to the same rating as blackpowder. You would use the same grade as you normally do in your gun. For most hunting muzzleloader rifles, that is FFg.

Note that Pyrodex is graded a little differently. RS grade is for rifle and shotgun use, while P is designed for pistols. "Select" is a premium grade of RS that is more carefully screened for kernel size.

PELLETS

In 1997, Hodgdon introduced Pyrodex pellets that are a solid form of Pyrodex. Designed for use in in-line rifles only, the pellets are available in two weights for .50 caliber: 30-grain and 50-grain. In .54 caliber, pellets are offered in 60-grain. You simply select the combination you need to make your desired charge weight. This eliminates the problems of measuring and pouring each charge. Each pellet has an ignition pad on one end that is a darker black; this should be loaded pointing at the back of the gun.

In a few short years, the pellets have become the propellant of choice for hunters using in-line muzzleloader rifles. The speed, accuracy and ease of use has ensured that they will remain in that position. I use them almost exclusively when hunting with in-line muzzleloaders and sabot bullets.

The latest trend is for gun companies to offer "3-pellet" guns that are designed to be used with 150-grain equivalent charges. However, Hodgdon does not recommend that its Pyrodex pellets be used in any combination that exceeds 100 grains.

extreme conditions found while hunting. Of course, it can happen with blackpowder as well, but the odds of blackpowder igniting properly are better.

Any gun you plan to hunt with should be tested long before the season to identify potential problems. However, if you will be using any substitutes in a sidelock for any kind of hunting, make sure to test it extensively under a wide variety of field conditions. Just because things work well at the range all summer, don't assume they will when you are hunting. Lower temperatures and extreme weather can affect reliability.

While thousands of hunters use substitutes in their sidelock guns with total reliability and confidence every hunting season, I still trust blackpowder more in these guns. However, ignition has become almost a nonproblem with the more efficient design of the in-line, and Pyrodex has become the propellant of choice for most in-line shooters. With an in-line, particularly one using a musket cap or 209-shotshell primer, ignition with Pyrodex and presumably other newer substitutes is usually trouble-free. Even with traditional #11 caps, ignition problems related to the propellant are almost unheard of in a quality in-line muzzleloader.

All substitutes are measured by volume to duplicate blackpowder. That is, if your measure is set for 100 grains of blackpowder, it will give the equivalent of that in Pyrodex (or Clean Shot or Clear Shot). However, charge weights will be dif-

VELOCITY COMPARISONS

*D*o all propellants of equal charge and volume produce the same amount of velocity and energy? Does one powder "store" more energy in a given charge than another? Are the substitutes "just as good" as blackpowder?

There's only one way to tell: Shoot equal charges of them all using the same type of bullet, then measure the velocities. So I did just that, measuring velocity averages with currently available and appropriate propellants using today's three most common styles of muzzleloaders.

Clean guns were first fired with a fouling shot. Then the barrels were swabbed with a Thompson/Center Seasoning Patch treated with Natural Lube 1000 Plus Bore Butter. After each shot, another of these patches was passed through the bore. This cleaned the fouling from the bore and kept the bore condition consistent from shot to shot.

As the shooting progressed, fouling was noticeably reduced. This was due not only to the elimination of any petroleum products from the bore which can react with the powder to produce more fouling, but also to the "seasoning" of the bore with the natural lube. Although at the start of the test it was often difficult to pull the patch back out of the bore, by the end of the shooting, the patch passed through with ease. Fouling was much less pronounced and cleaning was easier.

All powder charges were measured by volume. Velocities were measured 10 feet from muzzle with an Oehler 35P Chronograph.

SIDELOCK

Even with the hot musket cap ignition, all the substitutes in powder form showed a tendency to hang-fire, confirming my belief that sidelock guns work best with blackpowder.

The Clean Shot pellets were surprisingly good at exhibiting quick ignition. However, velocities were erratic with the extreme spread over three shots at 220 fps. Considering that GOEX blackpowder showed an extreme spread of 2 fps and all other others were below 50 fps, this would seem a bit high.

Pyrodex pellets were erratic in ignition.

Does one powder "store" more energy in a given charge than another? See the chart at right.

However, it should be noted that Hodgdon does not recommend that the pellets be used in anything but an in-line muzzleloader. If a priming charge of FFFFg blackpowder was poured into the barrel before the pellets, ignition was usually very fast and consistent. Prior to loading the pellets, I used a Thompson/Center Flintlock pan charger tool to dispense 3.5 grains of Swiss FFFFg. When I did this, the Pyrodex pellets worked fine.

IN-LINE

Blackpowder showed consistent velocities, which is a precursor to good accuracy. Swiss blackpowder showed the highest velocity of any propellant tested.

Clear Shot pellets showed erratic velocities with an extreme spread of 339 fps when counting a "freak" shot of 1,737 fps. This shot was thrown out and was not included in the velocity average. Even without it, the other three shots still had an extreme spread of 73 fps which was higher than any other propellant tested in this gun except Clear Shot Powder, which had an extreme spread of 110 fps over three shots.

Velocity Comparisons

FLINTLOCK

Test Details

- .50 Caliber Thompson/Center Arms Hawken Flintlock
- 100 grains blackpowder charge by volume
- 175-grain, .490 Remington Premier Golden Lead Round Balls
- Thompson/Center Pre-Lubed Pillow Ticking Patches
- 28-inch barrel, 1:48 inch twist rate

Propellant Details	Propellant Category	Velocity*
GOEX FFg GOEX FFFFg Priming 3.5 grains	Blackpowder	1,637 fps
Elephant FFg Swiss FFFFg Priming 3.5 grains	Blackpowder	1,624 fps
Swiss FFg Swiss FFFFg Priming 3.5 grains	Blackpowder	1,876 fps
WANO FFg WANO FFFFg Priming 3.5 grains	Blackpowder	1,589 fps

*Note: Average velocity of five shots. Only blackpowder is recommended for use in most flintlock guns. Substitutes and pellets are not appropriate in this gun and were not tested.

SIDELOCK

Test Details

- 100 grains powder charge by volume
- CVA 295-grain, Hollow Point, Copper-Clad, PowerBelt Conical Bullet
- CCI — U. S. Musket Caps
- 24-inch barrel, 1:32 inch twist rate

Propellant Details	Propellant Category	Velocity*
GOEX FFg	Blackpowder	1,380 fps
Elephant FFg	Blackpowder	1,375 fps
Swiss FFg	Blackpowder	1,548 fps
WANO FFg	Blackpowder	1,344 fps
Clean Shot FFg	Blackpowder substitute, ball powder	1,439 fps
Clean Shot Pellets	Blackpowder substitute in pellet form	1,474 fps
Clear Shot FFg	Blackpowder substitute	1,242 fps
Pyrodex Select	Blackpowder substitute	1,419 fps
Pyrodex Pellets	Blackpowder substitute in pellet form	1,452 fps
Pyrodex Pellets With 3.5 grains of Swiss FFFFg primer	Blackpowder substitute in pellet form	1,457 fps

*Note: Average velocity of three shots.

IN-LINE

Test Details

- .50 Knight DISC In-Line Rifle
- 100 grains powder charge by volume
- 250-Grain Thompson/Center Arms Power Tip Express Sabot Bullet
- CCI #209 Shotgun Primer
- 24-inch barrel, 1:28 inch twist rate

Propellant Details	Propellant Category	Velocity*
GOEX FFg	Blackpowder	1,460 fps
Elephant FFg	Blackpowder	1,403 fps
Swiss FFg	Blackpowder	1,664 fps
WANO FFg	Blackpowder	1,416 fps
Clean Shot FFg	Blackpowder substitute, ball powder	1,374 fps
Clean Shot Pellets	Blackpowder substitute in pellet form	1,421 fps
Clear Shot FFg	Blackpowder substitute	1,298 fps
Pyrodex Select	Blackpowder substitute	1,496 fps
Pyrodex Pellets	Blackpowder substitute in pellet form	1,535 fps

*Note: Average velocity of three shots.

IGNITION!

You can be aiming the world's most beautiful rifle, loaded properly with all the best components, at a deer you've been dreaming about for a lifetime. But if you don't achieve ignition—which will light your powder or substitute charge and send the bullet on its way—you will go home empty handed.

Ignition is critical. In many ways, it's everything. Let's explore.

FLINTLOCKS

The modern muzzleloader hunter who wants a taste of the past may choose to use a modern reproduction of an old traditional flintlock gun. Or he may hunt in Pennsylvania where the law currently requires their use. Either way, a "flinter" is more reliable for hunting than most hunters believe.

The key to making flintlock ignition work lies in two things.

First, make sure that the flint is fresh and sharp and that it's adjusted to correctly strike the frizzen. Instructions for this are usually shipped with each gun. But lacking these, the most commonly accepted theory is that the flint should be inserted with the bevel down and held in the hammer jaws

with a piece of leather to cushion it against the metal jaws. It should be adjusted so that when the hammer is in the half-cock position there is a $\frac{1}{16}$- to $\frac{1}{8}$-inch gap between the face of the flint and the frizzen. The leading edge of the flint must be square with the face of the frizzen.

If the flint is all the way into the jaws and is contacting the frizzen, then it's too long and must be replaced. But if the gap is too big, the flint can be moved forward in the jaws.

You may wish to try dry-firing the gun a few times with no powder in the pan and without a powder charge or bullet in the bore. Watch to see not only that the flint is striking the frizzen squarely and is making contact all the way down the face of it, but also that the pan cover opens correctly to expose the priming pan.

The second thing—and this is where many new flintlock shooters go wrong—is the priming. The mistake a lot of hunters make is that they fill both the priming pan and the touchhole too full of powder.

The more priming powder in the pan, the more that needs to burn before lighting the powder in the touchhole. The priming powder in the touchhole then must burn through like a fuse to reach the powder charge. It works, but it's very slow and

Without reliable ignition, the rest is moot.

Contrary to popular belief, the touch hole in a flintlock should not be filled with powder. This pipe cleaner keeps the priming powder out.

it's likely why the flintlock has a reputation for hang-fires.

Some hunters are willing to put up with the longer ignition times as a fair trade-off for the reliability of stuffing the touch hole full of powder. In fact, Thompson/Center recommends this technique for priming its guns. Still, the priming pan should be only filled about half full, or to the bottom of the touch hole. After filling the pan to the bottom of the hole, the gun is turned so that some powder can trickle down into the touch hole. Striking the gun with the heel of your hand helps to "trickle" the powder into the touch hole.

Priming a flintlock. Most experienced flintlock shooters prefer that the priming pan be about half full of powder and that the touch hole be clear of powder. You should always insert the touch hole pick into the touch hole and run it in and out a few times before loading. This will ensure a clear channel. Leaving the pick in place while priming the pan will prevent the touch hole from filling with powder. Many shooters put a pipe cleaner or a nipple pick in the touch hole while charging the priming pan.

A shooter fills the pan about half full, to just below the touch hole level. (The old-timers used a feather, which they inserted into the touch hole and allowed the closed frizzen to hold in place.) Just prior to shooting, the shooter removes the obstruction, and the touchhole is clear of powder. This allows the fire to "flash" through the touch hole and light the charging powder instantaneously. If you doubt that it can happen that quickly, consider that one builder of custom flintlocks recently told me that when things are working right, the gun should fire before the hammer stops moving.

Powder choices. Only blackpowder should be used in flintlocks, because blackpowder has a much lower ignition temperature than any of the current substitutes. The grain size needed is determined by the bore diameter, just as it is with any muzzleloader. Most big game hunting flintlocks are going to be .50 caliber or larger, and FFg will be the most commonly used propellant. Remember though, the priming powder must be much finer grained. Generally speaking, in hunting guns the priming powder should be blackpowder and it should be FFFFg (four-F), as only this fine powder will ignite easily, quickly and reliably.

One exception to these "rules" currently is in the Thompson/Center "Firestorm" flintlock. This gun uses T/C's breech system with its "Pyrodex Pyramid," designed for use with Pyrodex pellets. The "Firestorm" breech plug is designed to provide a cone of fire that's directed at the pellet, and this flintlock rifle is actually recommended for use with Pyrodex pellets. However, the priming powder still should be FFFFg blackpowder.

T/C Firestorm flintlock.

PERCUSSION RIFLES

The key to reliable ignition from any percussion cap or primer is a clear channel to the powder. If there is nothing to impede the fire during its journey from the cap or primer to the powder charge, things usually work pretty well.

It goes without saying (or at least it should) that the nipple must be in good condition and the proper size for the caps must be used. It's foolish to try to stretch another season out of an old nipple. A nipple only costs a few dollars, and it's good policy to start each hunting season with a new nipple.

Replacement nipples not only aid in ignition, but in safety as well. An old "shot-out" nipple may have an enlarged ignition channel that is allowing too much blowback. This can be dangerous to the shooter or to any bystanders, as it can cause excessive gas, powder and pieces of the cap to fly off with enough force to cause injury.

Buy only quality, brand-name nipples and consider one of the designs that provides a "hotter" spark, like the Thompson/Center Hot-Shot Nipple.

An old and burned-out nipple will have a rough and eroded channel that will impede the fire. Any rough surface can have this effect, including poor machining that leaves tool marks or burrs either in the nipple or the gun.

Don't be a turkey—use a good nipple. I remember hunting turkeys once with an inexpensive imported muzzleloading shotgun that, to put it as delicately as possible, "lacked refinement." To compound the problem, we were shooting cheap, imported, percussion caps and charging the guns with Pyrodex RS. (Pyrodex is a fine product, but it is harder to ignite than blackpowder. In a marginal situation like this, that can be a problem.)

We were hunting a smart, old Eastern gobbler who had played the game for years and always emerged victorious. He finally came to check out the few soft clucks and purrs that were floating on the gentle breeze into his strutting area, but when he stuck his head up and looked at the empty grassy flat where a sultry hen should have been waiting, he decided he didn't like what he saw. He turned around and started off at a fast, choppy, ground-eating pace that every experienced turkey hunter is familiar with. I tracked his head with the shotgun's bead and pulled the trigger. The cap fired and I kept the bead swinging just ahead of his head.

Ice ages came and went, mountains erupted from the earth and eroded to flat plains, time passed in what can only be described as eons, and finally the gun fired. Because I did my part well for a change, the gobbler politely fell down and laid still.

My partner later commented that he had already started to pick up his equipment to leave when the gun fired. It was perhaps a world-record hang-fire, and without a doubt, I got lucky. I doubt the result would be as successful a second time. I also doubt that my heart could take the strain.

I spent a little time with that gun later, polishing and replacing a few key parts, including the nipple. There was a big burr in the ignition channel, and I am sure that was responsible for most of the problem. After I removed it and made a few other little refinements, the gun became disgustingly reliable.

Misfires. Perhaps the single most common reason for misfires (other than water or a faulty gun) is that the oil or cleaning solvent is not cleared from the ignition channel before loading the gun.

Clearing the ignition channel is a simple process. Some hunters like to flush the gun with isopropyl alcohol or some other nonresidue solvent. But it's easier to simply fire a few caps through the empty gun and "burn" the oil or solvent out of the channel. For the last cap, point the muzzle at a leaf or piece of paper. If it moves, the channel is clear.

A build-up of fouling in the ignition channel is another common problem. In a hunting situation, the ignition channel should be cleaned every few shots. If cleaning equipment is not available, at least ream out the channel with the proper size "pick."

Be careful that the ignition channel is not blocked with debris or particles from the previous cap. Sometimes the foil protector that seals the priming charge on some caps will block the nipple's hole, causing a misfire or hang-fire. Also, a wafer of the cap itself can be cut from the copper and plug the hole.

It's simple if you remember this: The fire has to get from the ignition source to the powder charge. Make that easy, and the gun will fire. Make it difficult, and disappointment will follow.

After a half-mile crawl through the sage, you want your rifle to go off at the moment of truth. Clearly this hunter paid attention to detail and had good ignition with his muzzleloader.

Types of Percussion Caps

There are several types of ignition sources in popular use today for modern muzzleloaders. Here is a rundown of the most commonly used.

#10 Percussion Caps

This is a smaller cap and is designed to be used on some imported revolvers. It is not commonly used much in modern muzzleloading hunting rifles.

#11 Percussion Caps

This is the most popular percussion cap in use for almost all types of modern muzzleloaders, including in-line, sidelock or bolt-action. These caps are reliable, inexpensive and are all any hunter needs for most applications, particularly if using blackpowder.

#11 Magnum Percussion Caps

This is simply a #11 with more priming compound for a hotter flame. CCI says that its #11 Magnum is 24 percent hotter than a standard #11 cap. The magnum caps are recommended for all hunting applications, particularly when using blackpowder substitutes that can be harder to ignite.

Musket Caps

Musket caps are very popular. They stay with the "spirit" of muzzleloading while providing a much hotter flame (about 700˚F hotter than a standard #11 cap) that many believe is needed for blackpowder substitutes or pellets. Also, because musket caps have more priming compound, the volume or the flame is much greater.

Musket caps use a different, much larger, nipple, but most modern guns now have the option of changing to them by simply installing a new nipple.

The musket caps come in both "winged" and "non-winged" versions. The winged version is easier to remove from the nipple; if your gun has enough clearance to use them, they are probably the best choice.

Today's muzzleloading hunter has many options in primers and percussion caps.

#209 Shotgun Primers

Many modern muzzleloaders, particularly in-line and closed-breech guns, use a #209 shotgun primer. This is the same primer that is used in most modern shotgun shells. The difference is that rather than fitting over the nipple like a percussion cap, the shotgun primer fits inside like a "plug." This helps form a tight seal in some guns where closing the action will force the primer in tighter against a taper. The downside is that primers can be hard to remove after firing. There are tools designed to pry the spent primers out of the breech, but be sure to bring at least two with you when hunting; I have broken several over the years. A stuck primer can ruin a hunt if you don't have the means to remove it. Knight Rifles created the D.I.S.C. rifle to overcome this problem and it is one of the nation's most popular models today.

The upside of using #209 primers is that they provide a very hot flame: hot enough to light any powder and probably wet newspapers if you tried.

Rifle or Handgun Primers

There are many different systems that use rifle or pistol primers. They are hot and reliable. The option of using "magnum" primers makes them even hotter. Because they also fit inside (rather than over) the nipple, most of the systems employ some means to hold the primer in place that often doubles as a weather seal.

Chapter 4

HUNTING WITH MUZZLELOADERS

Our ancestors used blackpowder muzzleloaders because they had to. No other guns existed. But remember. To our ancestors, the muzzleloader was cutting-edge technology, and it was the very best option for fighting or hunting. Today we use muzzleloaders because we want to. Certainly for hunting, they occupy a space well down the ladder of performance, and the days when they were "cutting edge" are long past.

Our reasons for choosing muzzleloaders are as varied as the hunters who believe in them.

One reason is more hunting time—muzzleloaders allow us to access the special seasons implemented for their use. Any die-hard hunter craves more time in the field. We use muzzleloaders for the challenge.

A single shot and the inherent need for a close target make muzzleloader hunting more difficult. It's a uniquely modern concept that many hunters voluntarily seek out more difficult situations in their big game hunting.

Finally, we use muzzleloaders to maintain or even strengthen our ties with the past. By using the guns of our great-great-grandfathers, we feel drawn to a simpler time, and we build a bridge of understanding that spans multiple generations. With a muzzleloader in our hands, we can catch a glimpse of what hunting must have been like when our country was new and exciting. We can use a muzzleloader as a time machine that travels back to the past and brings us along for the adventure.

DEER IN THE WOODS

*L*et's face it, most muzzle-loader rifles are used for the same thing—hunting whitetails—and everybody knows that most whitetails live in the thick woods.

The white-tailed deer is an adaptable fellow. He has managed to expand his range so that he now inhabits just about every kind of terrain found in North America. However, his preferred habitat is thick woods with lots of edge cover.

In this type of hunting situation, 100 yards is a long shot, and most deer are shot at 50 yards or less. The goal is to anchor the deer in or near his tracks or, failing that, leave a good (and short) blood trail to follow.

This is the kind of hunting that is custom-made for muzzle-loaders. It is what makes black-powder hunting fun and is the backbone of the sport. It's when we can use the guns we like rather than only the guns that we know perform best. The shooting is not tough and the target is not particularly large or hard to kill.

Theories abound about bullet performance. Some folks think that dumping all the energy in the animal is the secret. They want a fast, lightweight bullet that comes apart in the deer. After hunting deer with just about everything that shoots for the past 35 years and taking enough of the critters to count well into the triple digits, I humbly (well, okay, so my opinions are not so humble) disagree with that thinking.

The white-tailed deer is number one with big game hunters using muzzleloaders.

For years the author's deer gun was a Thompson/Center Renegade .54 caliber sidelock with a peep sight that he received as a birthday gift the first year his home state of Vermont had a muzzleloader-hunting season.

MUZZLELOADERS FOR WHITETAILS

For the best performance, I think that a muzzleloader or any other firearm should punch all the way through a deer, leaving a path of destruction and a big exit hole. When it comes to muzzleloaders, my taste in bullets runs to big, heavy, well-constructed bullets that are traveling at moderate velocity.

For years, my deer gun was a Thompson/Center Renegade .54 caliber sidelock with a peep sight. My wife gave it to me for my birthday the first year my state had a muzzleloader-hunting season, and of all the blackpowder guns I own today, it will be the last to go.

I cast my own 430-grain Maxi-Ball bullets and pushed them with 110 grains of GOEX FFg blackpowder for a muzzle velocity of 1,470 fps. It was never a spectacular "drop-them-in-their-tracks" performer, but no deer that was fairly hit ever escaped, and every bullet penetrated completely. It was—and remains—my ideal "woods" rifle for whitetails.

Sure, I am more likely these days to be using the latest stainless steel, synthetic stocked, in-line rifle, equipped with a scope and shooting sabot bullets. I claim that it's because I need to test what's new and because the market is dominated by these guns. And this fact is also undeniable: These new rifles are more efficient.

But deer hunting is supposed to be fun and challenging, and the Renegade brings both elements to the hunt. I try to carry it in the woods a time or two every hunting season.

My father-in-law, John Kascenska, is an avid blackpowder shooter who has been heard to comment, "I love the smell of white smoke in the morning!" He refuses to hunt with anything but a sidelock or flintlock and thinks that putting a scope on a muzzleloader is worse than passing gas in church. He may not get as many deer as those hunters who use the "latest and greatest" firearms, but nobody has more fun or a greater appreciation of accomplishment as he does when he shoots a deer.

CALIBERS, BULLETS & LOADS

I firmly believe that woods hunting muzzle-loaders for whitetails start at .50 caliber, and full caliber, soft lead conical bullets are always a good bet. But there is no question that today's hunter likes sabot bullets. The best for this chore weigh at least 300 grains and will expand to at least two calibers at muzzleloader velocities. They are also tough enough to hold together and penetrate well.

Forsaking raw performance for tradition says a lot for the nostalgia of hunting with a traditional muzzleloader shooting a patched round ball. If a hunter is inclined to try this style of hunting, there are few big game animals or hunting situations better suited than whitetail deer in the close shooting found in the brush they love to call home. You will need to choose your shots more carefully than if you were shooting conical or sabot bullets, but a well-placed shot through the ribs will prove again the one undeniable truth of muzzleloader hunting. Both modern and not-so-modern hunters know that thousands and thousands of whitetails have fallen to the simple round ball. That's not going to change just because we have newer and better bullets, in-line guns, #209 ignition or propellant pellets.

The chart on page 85 suggest a few loads for whitetails in the woods.

The author's father-in-law, John Kascenka, with a good muzzleloader buck. Sidelock or flintlock—and no scope—are his personal muzzleloading rules.

Many hard-core whitetail hunters believe that there is a lot to be said for the nostalgia of hunting with a traditional muzzleloader shooting a patched round ball.

Best Loads—Whitetails

Gun & Caliber	Bullet	Powder Charge	Velocity	Comments	Notes
.54 Thompson/Center Renegade	Thompson/Center 430-grain Maxi-Ball	110 grains GOEX FFg	1,470 fps	Good all-around load.	A
Remington M-700 MZ .50	Barnes 300-grain Expander-MZ	100 grains Pyrodex Select	1,520 fps	My favorite deer load with a sabot bullet.	A
CVA Apollo .50	Hornady .50 Great Plains, 410 grains	Pyrodex Select 100 grains	1,402 fps	Hard hitting, deep penetration.	A
Knight Magnum Elite .50	Hornady .44 300 grains, XTP Sabot	Pyrodex Select 100 grains	1,514 fps	One of the best "pistol bullets" for muzzleloader use.	A
Remington MZ 700 Youth	Nosler 250-grain Partition	Two 50-grain Pyrodex Pellets	1,650 fps	My 12-year-old daughter took her first whitetail with this gun.	A
CVA Youth Sidelock .50 Caliber	CVA CopperClad PowerBelt	80 grains FFg	1,300 fps	My 11-year-old son's gun of choice. Just like his Grandpa!	A
CVA St. Louis Hawken .50 Caliber	Hornady 177-grain .490 patched round ball	90 grains GOEX FFg	1,828 fps	Something about a traditional load.	CVA
Flintlock .50 Caliber	182-grain .495 patched round ball	90 grains FFg	1,920 fps	True tradition.	A
.54 Caliber	460-grain Flat Point Hornady Great Plains	100 grains FFg or equivalent of Pyrodex Select	1,320 fps	Hit them hard, remove all doubt!	H
T/C New Englander .50 Caliber	300-grain CVA Deerslayer Conical	90 grains FFg Blackpowder	1,473 fps	John Kascenska's "Middletown Mauler" deer load. Good load anywhere.	A
.50 Caliber	.444-grain Black Belt Flat Point	100 grains Pyrodex RS	1,286 fps	Deep penetration expected.	B
.54 Caliber	425-grain HP Hornady Great Plains	105 grains Pyrodex Select	1,400 fps	Big and deadly.	P
.50 Caliber	470-grain T/C Maxi Hunter	Two 50-grain, .50 caliber Pyrodex pellets	1,301 fps	Good .50 caliber load.	P

A – Data tested by author. B – Data from Big Bore Express. CVA – Data from CVA.
H – Data from Hornady. P – Data from Hodgdon-Pyrodex.

Prairie Game

We are talking whitetails, mule deer and antelope (not the African variety) here. The "plains game" part of it means that we are hunting in the open prairie of the North American heartland where the potential for a long shot (relatively speaking, it's still a muzzleloader, not a sniper rifle) exists.

The primary consideration is still being able to place a killing shot with absolute precision. But we are doing it from farther here than any other location for big game hunting on this continent.

We should weigh the requirements of a muzzleloader and must consider a flat shooting load that will increase the range we can effectively shoot. But at the same time, we cannot neglect the terminal ballistics and how well a bullet works after it hits the critter. Some "flat shooting" bullets are terrible on game and wind up wounding as many as they kill.

On the other hand, you do have to hit them to have any bullet work. And with the extended ranges, the odds go up with bullets that have flatter trajectories. Achieving a balance of the two should be the goal.

Your primary consideration is being able to place a killing shot with absolute precision, but you are doing it from farther away on the prairie.

PRONGHORNS

Hunting pronghorn antelope is as American as it gets. Actually, they are not antelope and are not related to any members of the group. The pronghorn is a unique animal that is the sole representative of the unusual family *antilocapra*. The first of these date back about 20 million years. Some were the size of jackrabbits while others were larger than our modern day pronghorn. What they all had in common was that they grew horns but shed the horn sheaths annually like deer shed antlers.

The pronghorn is not a large animal, and it rarely exceeds 150 pounds—100 pounds is more like it. They are built for speed and are lightly constructed with small bones. However, they have large lung and heart capacities—and a toughness that can make them surprisingly hard to kill.

They are the fastest animal in North America and perhaps the world. Some say the cheetah is

Don't wimp out and take the long shots at pronghorns. Work hard, get closer, make the clean kill.

faster, but others dispute that. No matter. With cheetahs hanging out in Africa, the pronghorn is faster than anything around the American West that might have a hankering to eat them. They depend on that speed and their incredible eyesight to keep them safe.

The speed is, for the most part, irrelevant to the muzzleloader hunter. An ethical hunter should not, under any circumstances, take a shot at a running, unwounded pronghorn. You simply can't depend on hitting the kill zone, especially with a muzzleloader. There are tales of hunters shooting at a buck leading the pack and a doe that is three animals behind him falls from the bullet. Nobody is good enough to hit running antelope in the kill zone every time with a muzzleloader. No exceptions.

Their eyesight, though, is another factor. They can see as well as a man with 10X binoculars. The "goats" I have hunted see better than any mammal I have chased. They live in the wide-open spaces and use that vision to their advantage. Getting close to them is tough, but not impossible.

Hunt hard, get close. The tales of ultra-long shots being necessary for hunting pronghorn are perpetuated by braggarts and other lowlifes lacking the hunting skills necessary to get close. These are the same slobs who would have you believe that you must shoot at antelope running because you simply can't get a "standing still" shot.

It simply isn't so. I have never shot a running antelope and have never shot one past 200 yards, even with modern rifles. The last antelope I took nearly made the Boone and Crockett Club record book. He was an old and experienced veteran that knew how the game was played, and I shot him at 125 yards.

However, anything past 100 yards can be considered long range for a muzzleloader; 200 yards is way too far. If he's beyond 150 yards, look for some hunting skills and use them to get closer.

It is, though, a good idea to plan on the longer 100-yard-plus shots, and to select a load accordingly. Always try to get close enough to smell their breath before shooting, but plan and practice for the longer shots. That way, if you simply can't close the distance, you can still ethically take the shot if the animal is within your pretested skill and power zone.

DEER

Although mule deer and whitetails on the open prairie can grow to be twice as big as an antelope, modern muzzleloader hunting bullet and load selection for deer is almost the same as it is for antelope. Except with deer, it is even more important to stick with bullets that are heavy enough to

For hunting mule deer on the open prairie, it's important to stick with bullets that are heavy enough to have a decent sectional density so they will penetrate.

have a decent sectional density for effective penetration. And it's critical to use only quality bullets designed for controlled expansion.

CALIBERS, BULLETS & LOADS

Don't be lulled by the come-on of ultra-high velocity with super-lightweight bullets. You still need a bullet that can do the job after it gets there. Instead, look for the middle ground: a bullet that shoots fast, flat and accurate, but with enough heft to perform on game.

In a .50 caliber gun, consider something like the Nosler Partition 250-grain, Hornady XTP 300-grain or the Barnes Expander MZ in 250 or 300 grain, all sabot bullets.

You might also consider pointed, plastic-tipped bullets such as the X-Tended Range Sabot bullet sold by Cabela's. In .50 caliber, they are offered in 180 grain, 195-grain, 215-grain and 235-grain. Also look at the spitzer or Polymer

Tip sabot bullets offered by Precision Rifle Custom Muzzleloader Bullets. These streamlined bullets cut the air well to retain velocity and energy downrange much better than blunter bullets. This translates into flatter trajectories and more retained energy downrange.

For deer and antelope, you might consider some of the better .45 caliber guns. Most of these bullets will be .40 caliber. The PowerStar .40 bullet from MTI is offered in 350 grains, while most other bullets will be lighter. However, don't go below 225 grains if you expect reliable terminal performance.

If you have a 3-pellet, 150-grain rated gun and it will shoot these 225-grain bullets accurately, this is the time to use it. You want to shoot as fast as you can without sacrificing the accuracy or the killing power of a decent bullet.

Best Loads—Pronghorns & Prairie Deer

Gun & Caliber	Bullet	Powder Charge	Velocity	Comments	Notes
.50	Nosler 250-grain Partition	Two 50-grain Pyrodex pellets	1,709 fps	Good bullet on game under 300 pounds.	P
T/C 209X50 .50	Barnes 250-grain Expander MZ	Three 50-grain Pyrodex pellets	2,107 fps	Very fast.	A
.50	Precision Rifle Bullets. 235-grain Polymer Tip Sptizer	120 grains of Pyrodex P	1,800 fps	Slick bullet that shoots flat and retains energy. Available from Cabela's.	PR
T/C Black Diamond .50	300-grain Power Tip Express	Three 50-grain Pyrodex pellets	2,021 fps	Polymer Tip bullet for good long range performance.	TC
MTI White .45	350-grain PowerStar	120 grains of Pyrodex P	1,592 fps	Long bullet for good penetration.	MT

A – Data tested by author.
MT – Data from Muzzleloader Technologies.
P – Data from Hodgdon - Pyrodex.
PR – Data from Precision Rifle Custom Muzzle Loader Bullets.
T/C – Data from Thompson/Center Arms.

BIGGEST BIG GAME

North American "big game" is a loose term that generally applies to anything larger than a coyote. However, as it's used here, the term refers to the largest North American species, specifically anything weighing more than 500 pounds. That would include moose, elk, grizzly bears, brown bears and polar bears. We might also throw in musk oxen and perhaps bison. Although few exceed 500 pounds, I would include black bears—not so much for their size, but because of their inherent toughness.

For North America's largest game, bullet and caliber selection is critical.

Complete penetration with a good diameter exit wound is important for tracking any bear that has been hit, so hunting black bears requires much the same from a muzzleloader as does hunting moose and elk. I think too that we can include wild hogs in this category, particularly those hunted for trophy quality rather than meat. The largest boars rarely exceed 500 pounds, but they are tough customers that are built like bullet traps. The heavy gristle shield that covers a boar's shoulders and ribs makes it tough for a bullet to penetrate.

Of the species mentioned, most hunters will likely never pursue the big bears or exotic bovines with muzzleloaders. But black bears, moose and elk are available and affordable for the masses. Moose and elk are a lot different from the deer most of us are used to hunting, simply because of their size alone. As I write this, I am still recovering from a grueling Alaskan moose hunt. Much of my

They don't come much tougher than grizzly bears.

weariness stems from the work necessary after the bull hit the ground. A single quarter of meat from a big moose will weigh more than the average white-tailed deer. Until you see a big bull moose or elk lying dead at your feet, you really cannot appreciate how truly big they are.

BULLETS ARE CRITICAL

When hunting any really big game with a muzzleloader rifle, you need to focus on bullet penetration. Elk, moose and many bears are big critters, much larger on average than deer.

Bullets that work well for deer and similar game can fail on the bigger stuff. Most deer bullets, particularly sabot "pistol" style bullets, are designed for rapid and large expansion. But because deer are relatively small, the bullets still have adequate penetration to exit on most shots. For truly big game, however, deer bullets often do not have enough penetration to reach the important stuff with sufficient energy remaining to create the havoc needed to ensure a killing shot.

Penetration is the number one concern when hunting big game with a muzzleloader, but it alone is not enough. The penetration needs to come from a large and well-designed bullet to ensure a big wound channel. For that to happen with a muzzleloader, you need the right combination of bullet diameter and weight.

To accomplish this with a muzzleloader it takes a large diameter, well-designed and heavy bullet that penetrates deep enough to ensure an exit.

Lightweight expanding sabot bullets are a poor choice here. Keep them for deer hunting. For the big stuff, use large full caliber conical bullets or specialty sabot bullets designed for deep penetration. It's probably best to avoid hollow-point bullets, because you don't want a

A conical bullet is much heavier than a round ball of the same diameter. This means the conical will carry more energy to the target and penetrate better.

lot of expansion. Better to choose a bullet with a large, flat nose that will cut and punch through tissue and still expand somewhat. With all else equal, the longer the bullet, the deeper it will penetrate and the better it will stay on track.

I suppose a large round ball might also be considered, and certainly a lot of big game have fallen to them over the years, but consider that a .54 caliber round ball only weighs 224 grains. Round balls are notoriously poor penetrators, and they have trouble tracking straight through game. Modern muzzleloader hunters are best-advised to avoid them for hunting any really big game.

Muzzleloaders depend on bullet diameter and weight for their killing power, so the bigger and tougher the game, the bigger the bore needed. A bore diameter of at least .54 is by far the best choice for game weighing more than 500 pounds. However, I recognize that the .50 bore is the most popular in muzzleloading today, and most hunters will be using that caliber. The upside is that most of the muzzleloading bullet design technology has been centered around the .50 caliber, so there are some good choices. A .50 caliber is certainly the minimum that should be used for big or tough game, and then only with careful attention to bullet design and with long, heavy bullets.

Any bullet should be pushed with a heavy charge of propellant. Regardless if you are using blackpowder, Pyrodex, Pyrodex pellets or one of the newer substitutes, you should use charges on the upper end of the manufacturer's recommendations.

Long, heavy, conical bullets will provide the best performance on the biggest of big game.

The moose is the largest in the deer family, and only the bison is larger in North America. Use enough gun and enough bullet!

MOOSE

Moose are simply big. A bull can weigh 1,500 pounds or more. Other than bison, they are the largest North American big game. They have thick hides, big bones and offer lots of "moose" to penetrate from any angle.

Moose have huge hearts, big lungs and a lot of blood in their systems, and they are slow to realize they have been killed. A bull moose has a lot of body mass to soak up bullet energy, and even well-hit bulls often stay on their feet for a while. The trouble is, these bulls seem to have a knack for using that time to extract a last revenge on the hunter. It seems like they always manage to make it to the worst possible place to die—usually in deep, cold water or knee-deep mud. If you haven't quartered a 1,200-pound moose while standing in ice water to your knees and sucking mud with every step ... well then, you probably haven't moose hunted much.

Hit them hard. It's a good strategy to shoot a moose through the shoulders. Try to bust some bones to take away the moose's support structure so he can't wander into some soupy nightmare. Just make sure you have enough gun and bullet to pull it off. Those bones are big and tough, and they hide under a lot of muscle.

Don't think that just because a muzzleloader bullet is big and heavy it will do the job easily. We have a tendency to compare muzzleloader bullets to modern rifle bullets. If our muzzleloader bullet weighs three times more than the bullets our .30-06 shoots, how can it fail to penetrate even a large T-Rex?

Don't forget that muzzleloader bullets are made from pure lead, a very malleable substance. They tend to flatten and mushroom when contacting things like moose parts, particularly moose bones. This reshaping eats up energy and creates bullets that are difficult to push through tissue, inhibiting penetration. Modern rifles use advanced technical bullets that perform in a much different way.

If you plan to shoot a moose in the shoulders, you might consider using a specialty sabot bullet with a heavy, hard-cast flat nose. I make my own using a 405-grain cast from an RCBS mold #45-405-FN. I size it, without lube or a gas check, to .452 inch using a long sabot. Or you can buy similar bullets from companies like C&D Special Products or Precision Rifle Custom Muzzleloader Bullets. Just make sure that the bullets are cast from a hard lead alloy such as linotype. This keeps them from expanding and makes them act like a solid.

In this case, the flat-nosed design is deadly enough without expanding, as long as the bullet is of a large enough diameter. Handgun hunters have used this design for years with good service, and I can tell you from experience that this style of bullet kills almost any game just fine. If you worry about the lack of expansion from a "solid," consider that in Africa, these flat-nosed bullets are the choice of many professional hunters, particularly on the big and nasty stuff.

If you are still not sure and insist on using an expanding bullet or any lead bullet, play the odds. When in doubt, shoot the animal in the lungs. If you put a big bullet through both lungs, you'll have a dead moose on your hands. You should just hope he decides to make his final resting place one that's dry and accessible. Use full caliber, heavy conical bullets, or heavy, controlled-expansion sabot bullets like the Barnes Expander-MZ in the heaviest weight available in your bore size.

I have always been a student of bullet placement, and nobody knows better where to shoot something than the guy who hunts that game the most. I remember asking a Newfoundland native where the best place to shoot a moose is. "Right when he's straddling the yellow line, boy," he said with a grin. Later I had a chance to pack a few moose out a few miles on my back, and learned he was right.

For the biggest game, a muzzleloader hunter must use big, heavy bullets and heavy powder charges.

Even a wimpy elk is tougher than any moose that ever munched a fern. Load up right!

ELK

Elk are smaller than moose. A big bull elk weighs perhaps 900 pounds, but even a wimpy elk is still tougher than any moose that ever munched a fern.

A bull elk may be pound-for-pound the most bulletproof ungulate in the mountains. Wounded bull elk are known for running to the next mountain range while lugging a bullet that wasn't quite in the right place or failed to penetrate. Elk are notorious for their determination and tenacity, and if you don't kill them well, they can lead you on a chase you will regret to your last breath. You must do the job right with the first bullet, because if you fail, there likely won't be a second chance.

Elk have thick hides that are often caked with mud from rolling in the wallows. Behind that hide are big, tough muscles and massive bones. A big bull can soak up a lot of bullet energy and "too much gun" is not something you ever need to worry about when hunting with a muzzleloader.

I still like the shoulder shot and also the heavy, hard-cast bullets in sabots. But heavy conical bullets are perhaps the best choice. You might consider a hollow-point conical, depending on the shot you expect to take. At the risk of boring you, I will again recommend a lung shot as the safest. If you are taking a lung shot, then a hollow-point conical bullet will offer a little expansion while still, with all likelihood, making an exit hole.

The elk will probably run off, but it will be easy to follow all that blood running out that big exit hole. If you put the bullet through both lungs, you will find a dead elk at the end of the trail.

Elk live, for the most part, in the high, steep mountains. It's a lucky hunter who follows the blood downhill. The closer to the bottom the elk makes it before he gives it up, the less you need to carry out on shaky knees.

Pound for pound, bull elk is the most bulletproof ungulate in the mountains. "Too much gun" is not something you ever need to worry about when hunting them with a muzzleloader. Take heavy bullets too.

Bears are North America's only true dangerous big game. They have the ability, disposition, tools and willingness to kill you. Keep that in mind when hunting them with a muzzleloader.

BIG BEARS

Any bear is a tough customer. Grizzly bears and brown bears are big, tough and dangerous when they are upset. Both bears are one and the same from a scientific standpoint. It's just that the coastal brown bear lives an easier life and over the years has evolved into a bigger bear than the grizzly. Based on weights, a grizzly is about twice as big as a black bear, and a brown is about three times as big. Polar bears weigh about the same as brown bears.

All these bears share a common bond in that they are North America's only truly dangerous big game. They have the ability, disposition, tools and willingness to kill you. It would serve you well to keep that in mind when deciding to hunt the big bears with a muzzleloader.

From the standpoint of what to shoot them with, we can consider all these bears as one and the same. They are big, tough, nasty-tempered and hard to kill. If you hunt them, it will be expensive, and it's unlikely that you will ever do much of it in your lifetime. You owe it to yourself and to the bear to show up well-equipped.

Simply put, use the biggest, most accurate muzzleloader you can find. Shoot full caliber conical bullets or hard-cast flat-nosed sabot bullets with lots of weight and a big, flat nose. Push them with all the power you can safely muster in that gun. And finally, aim carefully because you will only have one shot.

I have no first-hand experience, but rumor has it that an empty muzzleloading rifle is a notoriously poor gun for stopping charging grizzlies.

BLACK BEARS

For most of us, any bear hunting we do will be for black bears. To be honest, I think they are a much more sensible target for muzzleloading rifles than the big bears of the North Country. In many respects, the black bear may well be the perfect target. A lot of bear hunting is conducted from tree-stands while guarding a bait. Often criticized, but rarely by anyone who has done it, bait hunting for black bears can be heart-stopping excitement. If there is a hunting situation better suited to using a muzzleloader rifle, it has sure escaped my notice. Muzzleloaders and bait-hunting for black bears seem like the perfect couple.

It is often said that any gun that works for deer is fine for bears. Don't you believe it. It takes a lot more gun to reliably kill black bears than it does whitetail deer. Bears have thicker hides, bigger bones, bulkier muscles and an inherent toughness that deer simply don't possess.

When a deer is hurt, it's a sure bet that he will lie down before too long. A bear takes off with a destination in mind; he will either get to that place or die trying.

I have tracked dozens of wounded bears, and those we have found have either been dead or in a

In many respects the black bear may well be the perfect big game for a muzzleloader hunter.

Think of a bear as a big catcher's mitt for bullets: tough to penetrate!

hapless critter. Of course, the writer always qualifies that wish as impossible. He's right: It's impossible to design a bullet for that. But he is also wrong: The bullet would be far from perfect. To have a big exit hole, the bullet has to exit with plenty of velocity and energy remaining. Our writer's "perfect" bullet would make a hole smaller than the bullet.

Think of the hide as a big catcher's mitt designed to stop bullets. Didn't you ever wonder why so many bullets are found just under the hide on the off side? The hide will stretch out and stop the bullet, unless it has enough remaining energy to penetrate through. If it barely does this, the hide will stretch around the bullet before it can push through. Because hide is elastic, it will snap back, leaving a small exit hole. But the bullet that blasts through with lots of remaining energy and a large temporary wound channel caused by hydraulic action will blast a hole through the hide that is bigger and will leave a better blood trail. While some shooters think the remaining energy is wasted if the bullet has passed through the critter, it simply isn't so.

This blood trail is important because bear feet leave subtle tracks that are hard to follow; a blood trail is usually your only hope of following the bear after the shot. Bears are also tough. Most will run at least a little when hit with any gun.

Shot placement is key. The kill zone on a bear

damn good hiding place. I have never found one still alive that was bedded in the open.

I have weighed a lot of black bears; most are a lot smaller than people think. The majority of black bears shot are less than 250 pounds after field dressing. Many are less than 200 pounds. But you must plan for any bear that can show up no matter where you are hunting—even the bear that weighs an honest 350, 400 or even 500 pounds. Choose your gun, load and bullet for that bear and you won't be disappointed, no matter which bruin comes out to play.

Tough customers too. While black bears average only a bit more body weight than a large deer, they have physical characteristics that cause them to leave skimpy blood trails. Loose hides, lots of bullet-hole-plugging fat, and hair that soaks up blood like a sponge—all create the need for large exit holes to ensure good blood trails. That means the bullet must exit with lots of remaining energy.

You may have read often about the "perfect" bullet: one that passes through the critter, expending its energy until it barely has enough left to exit and falls to the ground just inches past the

This Maine black bear fell to a Remington MZ-700 rifle and a Remington Copper Solid bullet.

Hogs are nature's perfect bullet traps. You'll need big, heavy bullets. North American Hunter *editor Gregg Gutschow toppled this pig.*

is relatively small. Long hair makes a bear appear bigger than he is, and when it's hanging down it masks the true location of the bottom of his chest. Hunters will often shoot low. Also, from a tree-stand, the angle of the shot requires that the bullet entry be a little high. A bear's heart is low and farther forward than a deer's, and the bear's lungs are smaller. The target zone is actually smaller than what deer hunters are used to and a little more forward in the animal. It's best to try to shoot when the bear is slightly quartering away from you so you can hit both lungs, and to aim for the center of the bear (top to bottom), just slightly behind the shoulder.

On broadside shots, it's better to aim right at the point of the shoulder. Not only will you hit the lungs and possibly the heart, but you will also break one or both shoulders, helping to put the bear down more quickly. This is, of course, another reason to use a big, heavy bullet. Because bones are tough on bullets, inferior bullets can fail to penetrate after smashing through the shoulder. Shot placement is still more important than any other single factor with any game, but doubly so with bears.

Bullets for black bears. The best bullet for black bear hunting would probably be a full caliber, conical hollow point, but one with plenty of weight. You can also use a heavy sabot bullet, but only one with proper construction.

The hard-cast, flat-nosed bullets, of course, are good, but also consider the heaviest high-tech bul-

let you can find. The Barnes Expander-MZ is a good example. This solid-copper bullet expands to a remarkably large diameter, but it will penetrate better than a lead-core bullet of equal expanded diameter and weight. That's because the bullet splits into "petals" as it expands. The end result, viewed head-on, looks somewhat like a flower. The spaces between the petals act like "relief valves" to allow tissue to flow through as the petals cut through the critter. As opposed to the plowing action of an expanded lead-core bullet, this special splitting allows deeper penetration than one might expect, and creates a lot of damage.

HOGS

For the purpose of bullets, consider that hogs are like black bears. Any bullet that takes bears well will also take hogs. Big, heavy bullets are needed, but they can be of the expanding variety.

BISON & MUSK OXEN

Bison are just plain huge. On top of being huge, musk oxen live in the cold, where rifle performance will be degraded. Use deep-penetrating, hard-cast sabot bullets for either. It comes down to penetration, penetration and penetration.

No matter which big game you are hunting, don't be fooled into accepting the "high velocity" argument. High-velocity bullets might fly flatter, but they don't penetrate well. It's a muzzleloader. Use a heavy bullet. That's what they were made to use.

Bison are the largest critters in North America. When shooting them, it all comes down to penetration.

Best Loads—Biggest Big Game

Gun & Caliber	Bullet	Powder Charge	Velocity	Comments	Notes
Thompson/Center Renegade .54	Thompson/Center 430- grain Maxi-Ball	110 grains GOEX FFg	1,470 fps	Good all-around load.	A, E, M, LB, BB, B&M
Remington M-700 MZ .50	RCBS 45-405-Fn .451 hard-cast flat-nosed bullet in sabot	100 grains Pyrodex Select	1,370 fps	Excellent big game load for deep penetration.	A, E, M, BB, B&M, LB
CVA Apollo .50	Black Belt Bullets, 405 grains	100 grains Pyrodex Select	1,394 fps	Accurate bullet. Deep penetration.	A, E, M, BB
Knight Magnum Elite .50	Hornady .50 Great Plains, 410 grains	100 grains Pyrodex Select	1,335 fps	Suitable load for elk, moose and black bears.	A, E, M, BB
Thompson/Center Encore 209X50 Magnum	460-grain Maxi-Ball	3 Pyrodex pellets (150 grains)	1,752 fps	A big bullet going fast.	TC, E, M, BB, B&M, LB
Knight Disk Rifle	325-grain Swift A-Frame Sabot	100 grains FFg or Pyrodex Select	1,458 fps	Good sabot load with high performance bullet.	K, E, M, BB
Thompson/Center Big Bore	555-grain .58 Maxi-Ball	120 grains FFg	1,331 fps	A lot of gun is good!	TC, E, M, LB, BB, B&M
.50 Caliber	460-grain Flat Point Hornady Great Plains	90 grains FFg or equivalent of Pyrodex	1,320 fps	Heavy flat-nosed bullet. Good for big stuff.	H, E, M, BB
.50 Caliber	460-grain Flat Point Hornady Great Plains	100 grains FFg or equivalent of Pyrodex Select	1,320 fps	Big game—big bore.	H, E, M, LB, BB, B&M
.58 Caliber	525-grain Hollow Point Hornady Great Plains	90 grains FFg or equivalent of Pyrodex	1,275 fps	Use it because they don't make a .68!	H, E, M, LB, BB
.50 Caliber	.444-grain Black Belt Flat Point	100 grains Pyrodex RS	1,286 fps	Deep penetration expected.	B, E, M, BB

Best Loads—Biggest Big Game (continued)

Gun & Caliber	Bullet	Powder Charge	Velocity	Comments	Notes
.50 Caliber	460-grain TC Maxi Ball	Two 50-grain .50 caliber Pyrodex pellets	1,317 fps	Good .50 caliber load.	P, E, M, BB
.50 Caliber	490-grain Buffalo Bullet	90 grains of Pyrodex RS or Select	1,142 fps	Velocity a bit low.	P, E, M BB
.54 Caliber	540-grain T/C Maxi-Ball	120 grains Pyrodex RS or Select	1,396 fps	Hard-hitting for big game.	P, E, M, LB, BB
.54 Caliber	510-grain Buffalo Bullet	120 grains Pyrodex RS or Select	1,288 fps	Requires a fast rifling twist.	P, E, M, LB, BB
.54 Caliber	325-grain Barnes MZ Expander	110 grains of Pyrodex P	1,614 fps	Good for lung shots on moose, black bear and elk.	X, M, E, BB
.50 Caliber	600-grain Muzzle-loading Technologies Power-Punch	120 grains Pyrodex P	1,265 fps	If it walks on North American soil, you can hunt it with this load.	MT, E, M, BB, LB, B&M
.50 Caliber	400-grain Harvester Hard Cast	100 grains Pyrodex	1,375 fps	Deep penetration.	C&D, E, M, BB, LB, B&M
.54 Caliber	520-grain Black Belt Flat Point	Two 60-grain .54 caliber Pyrodex pellets	1,307 fps	Bullet no longer made.	P, E, M, LB, BB

A – Data tested by author.

BB – Suggested black bear load.

C&D – Data from C & D Special Products.

H – Data from Hornady.

LB – Suggested big bear load.

MT – Data from Muzzleloader Technologies.

TC – Data from Thompson/Center Arms.

B – Data from Big Bore Express.

B&M – Suggested for bison and musk ox.

E – Suggested elk load.

K – Data from Knight Rifles.

M – Suggested moose load.

P – Data from Hodgdon—Pyrodex.

X – Data from Barnes.

CHECK & RECHECK YOUR LOAD

*T*he deer had picked the location carefully. He was well-hidden, bedded in the thick hemlock trees at the crest of the hill. Only a hunter intent on moving deer would be likely to try fighting through this mess. Most hunters would walk on past in the more open hardwoods on the slope of the hill. I am sure that during the course of the past several weeks, this old veteran had lain quietly in his bed and watched a lot of hunters pass by, some no doubt within spitting distance of his hideout.

The deer had also planned that if he were discovered, escape would be available in any direction. All he needed to do was plunge off any side of this small knob, keeping it between the hunter and himself. It was almost foolproof.

Except that by the time the late muzzleloader season rolls around, most any deer still alive is practicing the same tactics and those hunters who wish success know they must force the deer to move. One hunter alone didn't have a chance with this buck, but two working together might.

This time, it was my turn to drive, and I knew from years of hunting this farm that it's a rare day when a deer isn't bedded on this hill. Because it was my buddy's family farm and he grew up rambling these woods, he thought he knew exactly where the deer would go if I approached from the east and let him get a whiff of me. As I topped the hill with the wind at my back, I spotted a flash of brown and I knew my friend was right.

I held my breath and waited while trying to suppress a smirk. We had outwitted this buck and he didn't know it yet, but he was as good as dead. I love it when a plan comes together!

Instead of the expected boom all I heard was a loud crack. I thought it was a stick breaking and concluded that the deer had seen my pal and had run off in a panic. But when I got to his stand, he had a sheepish look on his face, and I knew something was up.

Trying to run a farm, keep a fleet of log trucks working and do a little deer hunting is an exhausting way to spend the fall, and my buddy had been

If a buck like this escapes because you forgot to load your gun, the moment will stay with you for a long time.

a little late waking up that morning. He had grabbed his gun, a cup of coffee and jumped in my truck while still tying his boots.

In the confusion he forgot that he had unloaded his muzzleloader and cleaned it the day before. Usually if the weather is dry, he will hunt several days with the same charge in the gun. But the night before, he had shot the gun to empty it and then cleaned it before standing it by the wood stove so that it would be completely dry and ready to reload in the morning. The trouble is, he forgot that last part. The "crack" I heard was the percussion cap firing into the empty barrel.

"I had that deer in the cross hairs at twenty yards," he said. "You should have seen the look on his face when that cap went off!" That was several years ago and I have never known that hunter or that buck to make the same mistake again.

MAKE A WITNESS MARK

The moral of the story is to check and double check everything—and then check everything

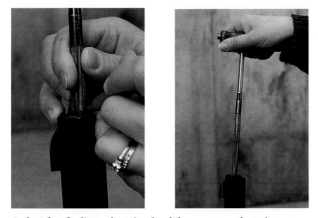

Left: After finding a hunting load for your gun that gives you the performance expected, you make a "witness mark" on the ramrod. This tells you at a glance if the gun is correctly loaded. Right: The mark on this rod is far above the barrel, indicating a serious problem. In this case, the gun has been loaded twice. Shooting it could prove disastrous.

again several times during the hunt. My buddy would have known at a glance that he had forgotten to load the gun. All had to do was run his ramrod down the barrel and see if the mark for his load lined up with the muzzle, indicating the correct load was in place.

The way it works is this: After you find a hunting load for your gun that gives you the performance you expect, make a "witness mark" on the ramrod. This tells you at a glance if the gun is correctly loaded.

To make a witness mark, load the gun, but do not put a cap on the nipple. Do this with a clean bore and make certain that the bullet is seated fully on the powder charge. Run the rod down until it rests on the top of the bullet. Place a permanent felt marker on the top of the barrel so it will mark the rod flush with the muzzle, and turn the rod to make a ring around the outside that is exactly flush with the muzzle. Now, after loading, you can easily see that the bullet is seated all the way down and that the correct powder charge is in place.

If you forget any component, or worse, double-charged the gun, the witness mark will make it instantly apparent. The witness mark will also tell you if the bullet has slipped forward in the bore during the course of the hunt. This slippage can happen easily, and shooting with the bullet forward, off the powder charge, can be dangerous and can ruin the gun. So check your witness mark every so often while you are hunting. It only takes a second.

Any time you switch loads, remove the mark with steel wool and make a new mark on the rod.

USE YOUR WITNESS MARK

Remember: The witness mark is only good if you use it. All my life I have had the habit with any firearm of checking to see that the safety is on every time I pick up my gun or shift it in my hands. I also check it every few minutes while holding the gun, regardless if I am walking or standing. I habitually check the safety hundreds of times a day. I have found it in the off position many times over the years. This usually happens from the safety catching on brush or my clothing. No rifle is immune to it happening. But because I am in the habit of checking so often, the safety is never off for long.

I have also developed the habit of checking my "witness mark" about a half-dozen times a day to confirm that my gun is correctly loaded and that the bullet is seated against the powder. I have learned to do this quietly and with a minimum of motion, and I do it only when I am sure it won't spook any game. It only takes a second or two, but it helps to keep things safe, keeps me confident, and makes sure that when a chance arrives, things are ready.

I also check the cap several times a day, first, to make sure it's still there, and second, to make sure it's seated all the way on the nipple. I have on more than one occasion found the cap to be missing. I also have found the cap unseated from the nipple where a cursory visual check would make the hunter think it's properly in place. This condition can cause the gun to misfire, as will, of course, a missing cap. The time to find that problem is not when a deer is in your sights, but before.

A little obsessive behavior goes a long way in ensuring reliability in muzzleloaders.

This cap has fallen off the nipple while hunting. If the hunter fails to notice and tries to shoot a deer, he'll be disappointed.

Chapter 5

CLEANING A MUZZLELOADER

*B*lackpowder is thought to be called that because of its dark appearance, but anybody who has shot much of it from a muzzleloader rifle knows it's probably named for the color of your hands at the end of the day.

Let's face it: Blackpowder shooting is a messy business. But isn't that part of the appeal? If we are truthful with ourselves, we must admit that occasionally we would all like to regress to our childhood when we were "allowed" to get dirty because that's what was expected.

As muzzleloader shooters, we expect to get dirty, smelly and grimy. It's unavoidable, enviable and part of the process. No matter how "adult" we think we are, we can't change that one bit. So we wallow in the grime and relive our childhoods. As one of my shooting buddies said, "Ain't it great!"

But blackpowder is programmed to bring us back to the reality of adulthood by insisting that we take responsibility. The fouling from blackpowder attracts water, which causes rust and destroys metal. A muzzleloader must be cleaned every time it is fired or it will be ruined. We cannot take the "kid" approach of neglect. Forgetting is not an option. We must act like adults and take responsibility for cleaning up our mess.

BASIC CLEANING GUIDELINES

*T*ake care of your muzzleloader and it will reward you with years of faithful service. It won't make you rich, handsome or famous, and it can't bring a great buck to shoot. But your gun won't let you down when you need it, and that's worth a lot. Especially if you manage to find that buck on your own.

Any muzzleloader must be kept clean. But cleanliness is much more important for blackpowder muzzleloaders than it is for smokeless-powder firearms, primarily because blackpowder fouling is hygroscopic (attracts water) and will cause corrosion and rust even in today's stainless steel guns. Routine field cleaning is imperative, as is a total and complete cleaning after each shooting or hunting session.

While most guns share the same basic cleaning requirements, there are also some differences with the various designs. Many cleaning products on the market will work, but it would be folly for me to name specific brands here. Make sure that the cleaning solvents you select are designed for blackpowder guns. Most of the solvents remove powder fouling very well. If you are trying to remove other bore fouling—either metal from bullets or plastic from sabots—make sure the solvent you are using is designed for that purpose.

A muzzleloader must be cleaned every time it is fired, or it will be ruined. These antelope hunters know, and are taking care of business at camp.

TOOLS OF THE TRADE

A cradle to hold the gun during cleaning is very useful. While you can clean your muzzleloader with the ramrod attached to the gun, it's better to have a good quality rod specifically designed for cleaning. You will need tools to disassemble the gun. Most manufacturers supply these tools with the guns. As each gun is different, it's probably best to use those specific tools. If you lost or never had them, contact the manufacturer for your gun. You will find a listing of

Routine field cleaning is imperative, as is a complete cleaning after each shooting or hunting session.

You can never have enough muzzleloader cleaning supplies!

addresses and phone numbers for many gun makers in the back of this book.

All lubricants, thread grease and rust preventative should be designed and recommended for muzzleloader use. Petroleum distillates can increase powder fouling and should be avoided, particularly in the bore.

CLEANING A SIDELOCK

Most sidelocks are relatively easy to clean.

First, make sure the firearm is unloaded and the cap is removed. Then cock the hammer, knock out the barrel wedge(s) and remove the barrel.

Fill a small bucket with hot water (the hotter the better). Squirt in some dish soap and insert the back of the barrel into the bucket. Wet a tight-fitting patch in the water and put it over the jag on your cleaning rod. It is important that the patch fit the bore tightly so that it creates a seal. Run the patch down the barrel. You should see air being pushed out of the submerged nipple.

Now slowly draw the rod up until the patch reaches the top of the barrel, but do not pull it out. This sucks the hot, soapy water in through the nipple and fills the barrel. As you push the rod back down, you will see the black water spraying out of the nipple and back into the bucket.

Repeat this several times, changing patches at least once. You will notice that the hot water is heating the barrel. After you finish, drain the barrel and wipe the outside with a paper towel. Run a couple of dry patches down the bore to dry the inside and then prop the barrel with the muzzle down to let it drain. The heat in the metal will aid in drying the water.

The hammer should be cleaned with an old toothbrush and either solvent or the hot, soapy water.

Clean the lock by spraying cleaning solvent into it and letting it drain out, flushing all the gunk with it. Follow by spraying a degreaser then, after letting that dry, lightly spray with a combination rust preventative and lubricant that is not temperature sensitive. It's best to remove the lock before cleaning, but if the lock is still in the stock, make sure to hold the gun so that the solvent does not drain into the stock.

Left: Plain ol' soapy hot water is one of the best "solvents" for cleaning blackpowder fouling. Right: As you push the rod back down you will see the black water spraying out of the nipple and back into the bucket.

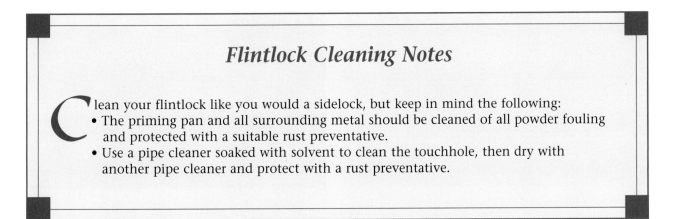

Flintlock Cleaning Notes

Clean your flintlock like you would a sidelock, but keep in mind the following:
- The priming pan and all surrounding metal should be cleaned of all powder fouling and protected with a suitable rust preventative.
- Use a pipe cleaner soaked with solvent to clean the touchhole, then dry with another pipe cleaner and protect with a rust preventative.

This is all the cleaning you need most of the time. When the barrel is dry, spray all metal inside and out with a blackpowder-recommended protectant. Again, don't use petroleum-based solvents, because they will react later to create more fouling.

Heavy-Duty Cleaning. Sometimes a more complete cleaning is called for, particularly when you are planning to store the gun for a while. Plug the nipple and fill the barrel with blackpowder solvent, then let it stand and soak for a few hours before draining.

It's a good idea to use a brass breech plug scraper to scrape the accumulated fouling from the bottom of the barrel where the powder charge rests. Then scrub the bore with a bronze brush wet with solvent, followed with wet patches and finally dry patches.

This will remove powder fouling, but not metal or plastic fouling, which can build up over time. You should be able to see this fouling in the barrel by using a bore light. If fouling is present after the barrel is dry, you should use a bronze brush and the proper solvent designed to remove the type of fouling in the barrel. Follow with solvent-soaked patches and finally dry patches. Remove the nipple and clean it with solvent and an old toothbrush. Clean the nipple channel with a cotton swab wet with solvent. Coat the nipple threads with grease before replacing it.

Dry the bore with dry patches and then spray it with a recommended blackpowder metal protectant. Make sure that you spray protectant into the nipple channel to prevent it from corrosion. (But do not forget to clean it out before loading the gun again.)

CLEANING AN IN-LINE

For reliable service, the action of any in-line muzzleloader must be disassembled and thor-

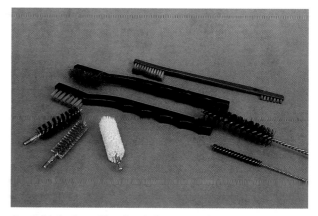

A good selection of brushes is important for cleaning all the rifle's nooks and crannies, as well as the bore.

oughly cleaned after an extended shooting session, as well as before and after the hunting season. With the design of most in-lines, the striker slides in the receiver, and as fouling from gases that escape the nipple accumulate, the striker movement can slow or lock up, causing misfires. (It is also important to keep snow, ice or dirt from building up while hunting and causing the same problem.)

Most in-lines have a screw-in breech plug and nipple that can be easily removed. Remove the nipple first, as it may be hard to remove from the breech plug if it's not in the gun. Soaking these parts in a good cleaning solution and working them over with an old toothbrush will remove most fouling. Be sure that the ignition channel is clear and clean; use pipe cleaners for that chore. Use cotton swabs or a brush made for that particular gun to clean inside the breech plug. Now give the striker the same treatment, making sure that the fouling is cleaned away.

The barrel and action can now be cleaned from the breech. With the plug removed, the bore is vis-

This bore light (shown next to a bullet for perspective) can be dropped down the bore and will allow inspection.

You must take an in-line's action apart and clean it after each shooting session.

ible so you can see if it is clean. Use a powder solvent, and if lead or plastic fouling remains, use a bronze brush with solvent designed for removing the fouling caused by bullets or sabots.

When replacing the nipple and breech plug, always cover the threads with grease to ensure you can take it apart the next time. Lubricate the striker with a good all-temperature liquid lubricant (do not use grease). The outside metal can be protected with a quality metal protectant and rust preventative that is recommended for blackpowder use. Apply a nonpetroleum-based protectant to the bore.

The trigger assembly should be cleaned. This is best accomplished with a spray cleaner. Take the gun outside for this chore, as the process makes a mess and some of the solvents used are nasty. Spray the trigger well, letting the solvent run out, flushing out the fouling, dirt and grease with it. After allowing it to dry, spray the trigger assembly lightly with a combination rust preventative and lubricant. Make sure that it is not temperature sensitive, or you may find yourself in trouble if it hardens in cold weather.

One nasty trait of most in-line guns is that with every shot, fouling gases spray on the bottom of the gun's scope. Use an old toothbrush and solvent to clean the gas residue from the scope and the mounts.

CLEANING BRASS & WOOD

By the time hunting season is over, the brass on your traditional muzzleloader may be looking a little like scrap metal. You can clean it up with brass polish, which is available at hardware stores. Simply follow the directions on the can.

As for wood: Take the stock off your gun and clean any dirt or debris from it with hot, soapy water. Do not immerse the stock into water. Dry the stock well near a mild heat source, at least overnight. Rubbing with a cloth wet with linseed oil will restore all but the most disgusting stocks. For those stocks, you might consider a total refinishing job. Sure, it's a lot of work, but what else do you have to do in the winter?

Bolt Action Cleaning Notes

Bolt-action muzzleloaders must have their bolts disassembled and cleaned every time the gun is cleaned. Remington's muzzleloader repair shop told me that the vast majority of problems they deal with are directly due to a failure to clean the bolt properly.

You must completely clean each part of the bolt and then lubricate it with a liquid lubricant that is not temperature sensitive.

Otherwise, clean your bolt action like you would an in-line.

Careful cleaning will keep your bolt-action muzzleloader working, which will make sure there's a big smile on your face after a buck enters your sights.

This inexpensive tool from Remington allows easy disassembly of the bolt on their muzzleloader.

Field Cleaning

Cleaning between shots is absolutely necessary if you are shooting plastic sabots. Although many shooters also recommend cleaning between shots for other types of bullets, find out if this is necessary for your gun simply by shooting it, both when cleaning between shots and not cleaning, to see which produces the best results.

There are a couple of ways to do this field cleaning. One way is to simply make a few passes with a patch that is impregnated with Wonder Lube 1000. I follow this with one pass with a dry patch, and then I load the gun. If I am hunting, I pop a cap or two to make sure the ignition channel is clear. I usually skip this step at the range and don't recall ever having a problem, but when hunting, I never take chances with something I can control. This method works very well from a shooting perspective. It also leaves a little residual lubricant in the bore to protect it from rust while hunting.

Another field-cleaning method is to swab the bore with presaturated patches wet with solvent. I usually use two patches, making two complete passes up and down through the bore with each. I follow with the same two dry patches. Then I pop two caps before loading to clear the ignition channel.

Regardless of which method is used, it's important to do it exactly the same way each time. Variations in the routine can result in bullet impacts that are not in the same place. After every ten shots, you should clean the nipple. This can be done by attaching a tube leading to a bottle of solvent. The sucking action of pulling a patch up into the bore sucks the solvent through the nipple, flushing the ignition channel. Always pop a couple of caps afterward to clear the channel.

In-lines should have their bolts cleaned periodically. Field cleaning can be accomplished by flushing with a spray solvent, followed by lightly lubricating the bolt. Or the bolt can be removed and cleaned with a solvent-soaked patch.

Cleaning between shots is recommended by many shooters.

Variations in the routine can result in bullet impacts that are not in the group.

The sucking action of pulling a patch up in the bore sucks the solvent through the nipple, flushing the ignition channel.

THE PYRODEX 8-MINUTE CLEAN UP

This is a fast and easy method to clean your muzzleloader after a day of shooting with Hodgdon's Pyrodex blackpowder substitute. Their Pyrodex EZ-Clean spray is formulated to attack the fouling left by Pyrodex. The spray also makes quick work of everybody's least favorite chore—cleaning up at the end of the day.

1. Unload your firearm and make sure no percussion cap is on the nipple. Remove the stock.

2. Spray Pyrodex EZ-Clean down the barrel and all over the rifle where powder residue is apparent. Use a toothbrush in hard-to-reach places. (Pyrodex EZ-Clean will not harm your gun's finish.)

3. Spray seven or eight large cotton patches until they are all well saturated.

4. Using the proper-sized jag and ramrod, put three of the saturated patches (one at a time) through the bore, running the patch in and out of the barrel five times each. Next, do the same with two dry patches.

5. Spray Pyrodex EZ-Clean on a brass bore brush and run it through the barrel five times.

6. Run two final saturated patches in and out of the barrel ten times; repeat the process with two dry patches.

7. Using two Wonder Lube-soaked patches, one at a time, swab the bore five times with each.

8. Wipe off the exterior of the gun with two or three patches that have been soaked with Wonder Lube. This will leave a thin coating of rust preventative on the interior and exterior of the gun.

Everything you need for the Pyrodex 8-minute clean up.

9. Clean the nipple with a nipple pick or pipe cleaner.

10. If you are cleaning an in-line that requires breech plug removal, use Pyrodex Lube to lubricate the threads of the breach plug after it has been cleaned.

11. It is a good idea to check the gun a week after cleaning. Run a Wonder Lube-soaked patch down the bore to check for rust.

Before loading, run a dry patch down the barrel to remove any residue. Then clean the nipple with a nipple pick or pipe cleaner.

Fire two percussion caps just before loading, or clear the flash channel of moisture and oil with degreaser spray.

(This clean-up process courtesy of the Hodgdon Powder Company.)

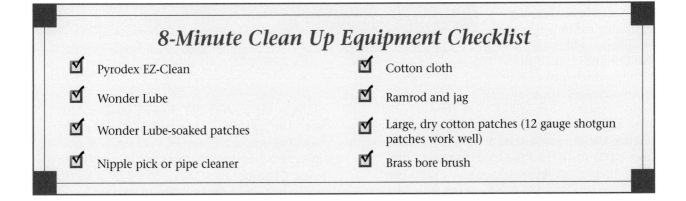

8-Minute Clean Up Equipment Checklist

☑ Pyrodex EZ-Clean

☑ Wonder Lube

☑ Wonder Lube-soaked patches

☑ Nipple pick or pipe cleaner

☑ Cotton cloth

☑ Ramrod and jag

☑ Large, dry cotton patches (12 gauge shotgun patches work well)

☑ Brass bore brush

To Clean or
Not To Clean

The question of cleaning between shots is simple if you are shooting sabot bullets. The answer is yes; you must clean between shots for any kind of decent performance. You can get away with a fast second-shot reload in a hunting situation, but try going without cleaning for three or four shots and you will find that it's going to be hard to make the bullet go down the barrel. Accuracy will also suffer.

With all other bullets, the answer varies.

Some conical bullets, like the Black Belt Bullet from Big Bore Express, the PowerBelt Bullet from CVA and the White PowerPunch Bullet, actually depend on a fouled bore to work correctly. The manufacturers all recommend that you fire a squib load of powder only before loading the gun for the first time so that the bore is fouled.

The reason is twofold: First, you will be shooting all subsequent bullets from a fouled bore. This makes sure that the first is on equal footing, which improves shot-to-shot accuracy. The

If you are shooting sabot bullets, you must clean between shots for any kind of decent performance.

second reason is that, unlike other conical bullets, these bullets are not designed to engage the rifling when loading. Instead, they are slightly smaller (about .001 inch) than the land diameter. This allows them to easily load, even in a fouled barrel. When the gun fires, the inertia of the sitting bullet will resist the push of the burning powder. This causes the bullet to "bump up" or obturate to fill the rifling grooves. However, because they are slightly smaller than the bore right up until the moment the gun fires, they depend on a fouled bore to help hold the bullet in place after loading.

Some conical bullets like (above, left to right) the PowerBelt bullet from CVA, the White PowerPunch bullet and the Black Belt Bullet from Big Bore Express, actually depend on a fouled bore to work correctly.

The lube you use on conical bullets and round ball patches can make a difference. I can remember my .54 caliber T/C Renegade becoming hard to load after several shots using Maxi-Balls and the lube of the day. I tried cleaning between shots, but accuracy was not quite as good. Also, I found that with a clean, lubricated barrel, the bullets would sometimes slip ahead in the barrel while I was hunting.

It always seems to be snowing or raining during our muzzleloader season, and the problem with a fouled bore is that it can be susceptible to rust and corrosion when hunting. So after loading, I made a pass with a patch that was covered with bullet lube to coat the bore with the lube. As long as I sighted in the gun with this same method, it worked pretty well.

But the new bullet lubes make the chore even easier. The staff at Ox-Yoke Originals actually fired

Run a patch soaked with Wonder Lube down the barrel after loading, to protect the barrel against the weather.

a Thompson/Center New Englander more than 1,000 times without cleaning. They used a lubricant that they call Wonder Lube 1000 Plus. Thompson/Center sells it as Natural Lube 1000 Plus Bore Butter. Several other companies market it under other brand names. None of the companies will tell me what's in the lube, but the package says it's food grade and it smells good enough to eat.

If you follow the directions and use this as a bullet or as a patch lube with conical bullets or round balls, fouling will be reduced, and you can shoot without cleaning for many more shots. Adding one of the Wonder Lube-soaked patches or "buttons" over the powder wads will help even more. It can also enhance accuracy.

I still run a Wonder Lube-soaked patch down the barrel after loading to protect against the weather, and I always make my final sight adjustments using that loading technique.

The lube you use on conical bullets and round ball patches can make a difference in how hard you have to work to clean your rifle.

Chapter 6

GEAR, GADGETS & GOODIES

A muzzleloading rifle is a relatively bare-bones piece of machinery—functional and simplistic in design and often a bit boring. Muzzleloader hunting, though, appeals to most of us "big kids" because it opens the door for lots of exciting and "necessary" toys!

Gear, gadgets and goodies are all part of modern muzzleloader hunting. They help us become better hunters, but the appeal is far more basic than that. It allows us to regress to that one magic Christmas morning that's in every childhood when everything was perfect and the tree was resting on a heap of presents that included almost everything you wanted.

Muzzleloading lets us collect things that we might not otherwise have, and it gives us an excuse to indulge our passion for "stuff."

And don't kid yourself with delusions of a "simpler" time and people. If Daniel Boone were alive today, you can bet he would have a bunch of speed loaders and a good capping tool in the pocket of his buckskins. I'll bet his "smoke pole" would have a scope on it too. 'Cause I know ol' Dan was my kind of guy—a guy who probably loved his toys.

MUZZLELOADER SIGHTS

The most accurate muzzle-loader in the world is only as good as its sights. If you can't see and aim with a degree of precision, the gun is worthless. It comes down to a matter of perspective. Accurate sights mean something different to a hardcore traditional shooter than they do to a modern in-line shooter.

PRIMITIVE SIGHTS

Generally, these are simple, open, iron sights. (Well, actually, they are made of steel, but the term "iron sights" has come to mean non-optical sights.)

With primitive sights, the elevation is adjusted by filing the front sight down until the gun is hitting where you want. This is a slow and tedious task with little room for error. It's a "one shot" deal, so it's best to know what you are doing. Even at that, having an extra front blade on hand is helpful. Usually

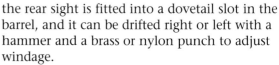

The most accurate muzzleloader in the world is only as good as its sights.

the rear sight is fitted into a dovetail slot in the barrel, and it can be drifted right or left with a hammer and a brass or nylon punch to adjust windage.

A "primitive" sight usually uses a very fine, small front sight. This aids in aiming precision, especially on targets, but the front sights are hard to see, particularly under hunting conditions. Only a hard-core traditionalist would select these sights for hunting, and he is probably experienced enough to understand what he is getting into.

ADJUSTABLE OPEN SIGHTS

Again, this is a blade or bead front sight and an open rear sight. They are the most simplistic of aiming devices and the most difficult to use. The difference is that the rear sight is fully adjustable by some means, usually by a couple of screws that move the sight right and left as well as up and down.

Often, adjustable sights will be a

Primitive sights are simple, open, iron sights.

Adjustable open sights come installed on most new guns.

little more advanced in design than traditional, primitive sights. The front sight will be larger and more sharply defined when looking at it. The rear sight will usually be a sharper profile, often with simple square angles that correspond with a blade-front sight's shape.

These sights come installed on most new guns because they don't cost a lot. Young eyes can use them reasonably well. But they are not the best, or even high on the list, as good hunting sights.

Open sights require the shooter to use three separate points: the rear sight, the front sight and the target. The human eye is not capable of focusing on all three, and to shoot well you must keep the front sight in sharp focus. In addition to the obvious aiming problems this creates, is that it causes the target to "blur" out. That's fine if you are target shooting, but when you are hunting, it would be better to keep watch of the animal. You want it in sharp focus so that you can stay attuned to any body language or a change in position.

Fiber-Optic Sights

One style of open sights that is showing up on a lot of muzzleloaders these days are fiber-optic sights. These use a light-gathering, colored fiber that has the end facing the shooter's eye. The front sight will have one round fiber and the rear sight will have two, which are separated by a space. The front and rear sights will use contrasting colors. For example, the front sight may be

green while the rear sight's two dots are orange. The fibers gather ambient light and will glow on the ends. The eye sees three dots and can line them up to shoot.

They actually work rather well if correctly designed. However, some guns are shipped with sights using larger fibers that were designed for hunting turkeys with shotguns. They often nestle the front bead on top of the two closely spaced rear beads. Because they are so large and because of this style of alignment, these sights make any kind of precision aiming all but impossible. It is better to have the type of sights using small fibers incorporated into iron sights and designed to line up all three dots evenly.

Fiber-optic sights use light-gathering, colored fibers.

Peep sights use the concept that the human eye looking through the hole will automatically center the front sight bead.

PEEP SIGHTS

A peep sight uses a round aperture for a rear sight and usually a bead front sight. The concept is that as the human eye looks through the hole that forms the rear sight, it will automatically center the front sight bead. This allows the shooter to ignore the rear sight and concentrate on the front sight.

Peep sights are much faster and easier for most shooters to use because they do not require that you make a conscious effort to maintain alignment between the two sights, only that you

look through the rear sight and place the front bead on the target. The eye must still remain focused on the front sight, so all the problems associated with that are still relevant.

Peep sights are much easier for my forty-something eyes to use than open sights. However, even when I was young enough to have the visual acuity of a hawk, I still preferred them to open sights. A peep is faster and easier than an open sight, and I don't think that's debatable.

By adding a fiber-optic front sight, the peep sight option becomes even more of a viable hunting sight for those places that do not allow optics, or for those hunters who prefer not to use optics on their muzzleloaders.

SCOPES

The argument often heard against scopes on muzzleloaders is that it makes them "too accurate." But that is, at best, a flawed argument. No scope can add to the accuracy of any gun. It simply makes guns easier to aim. While it can help the hunter shoot the gun more accurately, a scope or any other sight for that matter, does nothing to increase the inherent accuracy of the gun, nor does it get you within a good shooting range of an animal.

What the banning of scope use during muzzleloader seasons does do, though, is discriminate against older hunters or any hunter with poor vision. It also increases the incidences of wounding loss because shot placement is compromised.

Scopes are, in my opinion, the best option on

Peep sights work, whether your eyes are young or old. One careful shot from just over 100 yards dropped this whitetail doe where she stood.

Many of today's in-line muzzleloaders are designed for scope use.

relief is unlimited and there is no parallax. If you can see the dot and put it on the target, you will hit it. If you doubt they are very fast, go visit a handgun shooting competition where speed is the primary scoring system and see what the top competitors are using. There will be red-dot sights on virtually every gun in the winner's circle.

The Bushnell Holo Sight is similar in that it uses a holographic aiming point that is floated in front of the shooter's eye. It borrows from the "heads up" aiming technology of jet fighters. It's fast enough that I have successfully shot trap with one mounted on a shotgun.

With these systems, you can keep both eyes open and "see" the aiming point floating over the target. If your style of hunting calls for close shooting of any kind, but particularly quick shooting up close, check out these sights.

These sights are usually not optically magnifying, so they are legal in those areas of the country that allow optics, but not magnification, for muzzleloader hunting.

any rifled-barrel hunting gun, including muzzleloader rifles. Scopes magnify and brighten the image while putting the sights (crosshairs) on the same focal plane as the target, allowing both to stay sharp in your vision. A shooter with a low-power scope will always be a faster and more accurate field shot than the hunter who insists on using iron sights.

Scopes also enhance safety by increasing target identification. Sure, a scope looks (and probably is) out of place on a traditional muzzleloader, but on a modern in-line gun, it's by far the best option for sighting equipment.

ELECTRONICS

You might consider one of the many red-dot electronic sights or the Bushnell Holo Sight as an alternative to a scope or iron sights.

Both are extremely fast to use and can be a big asset for shooting at running game. The red-dot features an electronically generated aiming point that "floats" in the viewing area of the sight. Eye

Electronic red-dot sights are very fast to use.

MUZZLELOADING ACCESSORIES

uzzleloading is the last bastion of a "gadget freak." There are multitudes of gear, gadgets and goodies to use. Interest also ranges from the Spartan approach of a hardcore traditionalist to the "gimme one of each" attitude. (I'll confess to falling into that last category.) It would probably take a series of books to cover them all, but some accessories are important enough to detail here.

A **speed loader** is anything that holds a premeasured charge of powder and usually a bullet. Sometimes a cap is also included. There are a variety of these on the market. Some hold one charge, others hold multiple charges. Some speed loaders require a special tool to use while others work with your ball starter or ramrod. I prefer the latter, as it is one less thing to carry and remember. Some speed loaders even have a built in "short starter." Some are waterproof, others are not. Some are completely sealed, others use the bullet as a "plug" in one end. Most hold one shot, but some, like the Smart's Combo Muzzle Loader will hold several loads.

Every manufacturer says its speed loaders are the best, but what all speed loaders have in common is convenience—a hunter can load several premeasured loads before starting the hunt. Carrying several of these during the hunt elimi-

There are multitudes of gear, gadgets and goodies for a muzzleloader hunter to use.

The new "magnum" muzzleloaders designed for 150-grain or three pellet charges will require speed loaders designed to hold the larger charges.

nates the need to bring powder, powder measure, bullets and caps. They are, in effect, "cartridges" that provide one shot each.

It comes down to a personal choice as to the features, but every hunter should have at least half a dozen speedloaders. One hint: Charge them with fresh powder often, and never use charges from last year.

Another hint: If you are using a "magnum" muzzleloader with 150-grain charges, make sure they are large enough to hold that much powder before you buy.

Capping tools usually hold a supply of percussion caps and allow you to carry them in the field. But their most important function is that they aid

Capping tools come in many shapes and designs.

you in placing the cap on the nipple. One of the most frustrating experiences on earth is trying to place a cap on a tight in-line gun with cold, clumsy fingers when you have a deer hit and you don't know if it's down or needs shooting again. Using a capper makes this much easier. It's another "must have" for a modern muzzleloader hunter. There are many designs and somebody makes a capper to fit anything you are going to prime your gun with.

Pan Chargers. There is no need for a capper when you are shooting a flintlock. However, you do need something to carry the FFFFg priming powder. If that powder holder has the ability to dispense the correct

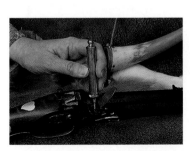

The pan charger from T/C dispenses just the right amount of FFFFg into a flintlock pan.

amount of powder into the priming pan, so much the better. T/C makes one that holds about 80 grains of powder and dispenses the correct amount to fill the priming pan half full each time you activate the dispensing tip.

You will need a **powder measure** for shooting or for filling your speed loaders. The best are adjustable, usually in 10-grain increments. Better

T/C blackpowder measure.

still are those calibrated in 5-grain increments. There are several styles available and it often comes down to a personal choice in the options you like. Some powder measures are stand-alone, while others are integrated with a powder reservoir so that you can dispense directly to the powder measure from the powder holder.

Hornady makes a bench-mounted model that can fill up a lot of speed loaders in a hurry.

Weather protection. Protection from the elements is covered elsewhere in this book. However, there are lots and lots of commercial products to help keep water and powder separated. Some work, some don't. They are too prolific to cover them all here. When you shop, remember the adage: "Buyer beware."

If your rifle has a muzzle brake, keep rolling out the muzzle mitt to cover the brakes.

A bullet centered in the bore when loading is usually more accurate. A **bullet alignment tool** is simply an attachment that screws into the end of the ramrod. It will have a contoured face to match the bullet profile and it will be bore diameter so that it rides on the lands and keeps the bullet centered. Barnes recommends using an alignment tool with its Expander-MZ bullets, and

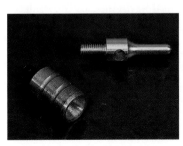

Bullet alignment tools help insure that the bullet is centered in the bore when loading.

so do I. Your accuracy will be noticeably better when you take advantage of this device.

A **patch puller** is an attachment that screws on to the rod and enables you to retrieve a stuck patch. If you don't have one, I'll guarantee there will be a time in your future when you will desperately wish that you did.

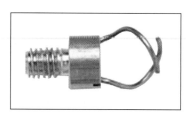

T/C patch puller.

T/C bullet puller.

A **bullet puller** is similar to a patch puller in that it's made to retrieve a bullet that is loaded without powder behind it. Most bullet pullers consist of a simple screw attached to a bore-sized guide that keeps it centered. You attach it to the rod and turn the rod while applying pressure so that the screw threads into the lead of the bullet. This allows you to pull the bullet out of the gun. A bullet puller is well worth the few dollars it costs. Carry it in the woods, because if you are ever going to load a bullet and forget the powder, it will be after you just shot at a deer and are reloading. There is something about the excitement that puts your brain in reverse.

It is dangerous to a bullet puller when you have a fully charged gun. Use other methods to remove a bullet if there is a powder charge behind it. Shooting at a safe backstop is the best and safest.

The screw-in style of bullet puller will not work with solid-copper bullets in an in-line, so other methods must be employed. Fire the gun into a safe backstop if there's a powder charge in the barrel. Remove any ignition device (cap or primer) and remove the breech plug, then push the bullet through, if there's no powder charge.

CO$_2$ Bullet Discharger. Another great method of pulling a bullet is found in the kits that allow you to inject pressure from a CO$_2$ cartridge through the nip-

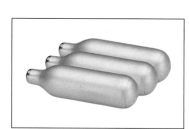

CO$_2$ cartridges.

ple to push the bullet out of the barrel. This is another tool that doesn't make its value apparent until you need it.

T/C breech plug scraper.

Breech plug scraper. In many sidelocks, the breech plug is not removable. A contoured scraper that threads into the end of the rod allows you to clean out the fouling that accumulates at the back of the barrel.

Jags are the attachments that screw onto the end of the rod and hold the patch for cleaning. Make sure you have the correct size for your gun. They also serve as a means to push the bullet with the rod while loading.

A selection of jags.

A **nipple pick** is a simple little tool that can make your life easier. Its sole function is to clear the channel through the nipple to the powder charge. It is nothing more than a small wire "nail" with a handle of some kind. Every shooter needs at least one. Having some back-up nipple picks is always a smart idea.

A **touch hole pick** is basically the same as a nipple pick but is

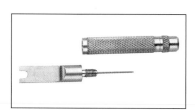

T/C 4-way combo tool includes a nipple pick, essential for clearing the channel from nipple to powder charge.

The touch hole pick is shown in the touch hole of this flintlock. Also note the brush for cleaning carbon from the pan.

A selection of ball starters. These "short" ramrods are used to start a bullet down the barrel.

designed to clear and clean the touch hole on a flintlock gun. A must-have if you shoot a flinter.

Ball starters. The "short starter" is, in essence, a short ramrod used to initially start the bullet. Because it's shorter and stiffer, it is easier to control than a full-length rod as the bullet or sabot is first engraved by the rifling. You can get away without one in an emergency situation by gripping the rod low, particularly if you are using sabots, which start easier than conicals or round balls. But why would you want to?

Also, it can be dangerous to try starting tight-fitting bullets with wooden rods. They can break and stab you with the jagged end. I once saw this happen while we were hunting moose in a very remote area of British Columbia. Fortunately, it only made a nasty cut on the hunter's hand. It could have been a lot worse and medical help was days, not minutes, away.

Usually, the **ramrod** that comes with the gun is fine for hunting. But for range shooting, you will want something better. A longer, stronger rod with a big, comfortable handle will make life much easier.

One-piece rods are stronger, while jointed rods are easier to transport. Regardless of which you choose, make sure you have a **muzzle guard/rod guide** and use it every time. This device fits into the muzzle of the gun and keeps the rod aligned with the center of the bore. Not using one can result

A muzzle guard bore guide centers the rod and prevents damage to the barrel's crown.

in rod wear on the crown, which degrades accuracy.

T-handle adaptors. A handle in the shape of a "T" that screws into the end of the rod on your gun enhances your grip. This is essential for pulling a tight patch and very helpful when seating bullets.

Sure, a wadded-up handkerchief will protect your palm while you seat a bullet, but the T-handle does it better.

A T-handle adaptor is better than a wadded up handkerchief to protect your hands while seating bullets.

You need something to carry all this stuff in the woods, don't you? I don't know why it's the called the **possibles bag**, but I suppose it's because you stuff as much as "possible" into it before you go

Nathan Towsley made this small possibles bag from tanned deer hide and a tanned squirrel hide.

A variety of powder flasks.

hunting. Or maybe because the idea is to pack everything in that you could "possibly" need.

Nylon is probably best, but leather is more traditional. Sure, you can use a fanny pack rather than the traditional over-the-shoulder single strap, but you won't look as cool.

Dispensing powder directly from the can is messy, wasteful and dangerous. You should transfer a smaller amount to a **powder flask**. Brass is the only metal to consider, because it will not spark. Most flasks have some sort of dispensing device and many have an integral powder measure.

Powder horns are the "low-tech" approach to a powder flask. They are available from commercial suppliers and custom makers, or you can make your own. If you are shooting with traditional equipment, it's not a law that you must use one, but it should be.

Use a patch knife to cut oversized patching material to size.

A **patch knife** is a small knife used to cut off excessive patching material. If you are using precut patches, you don't need a patch knife. If you are patching balls with your shirttails or your wife's bedspread, this is a pretty handy accessory.

A **wedge pin puller** is one notable tool that's handy beyond its cost when you are taking a sidelock gun apart for cleaning.

Wedge pin puller.

T/C deluxe "universal" nipple wrench.

To correctly clean any muzzleloader, it must be disassembled. Remember, the first rule of craftsmanship is to use the "right tool for the job," so make sure you have the correct wrenches—including a **nipple wrench** and breech plug wrench—and tools to reduce your particular gun to its base parts.

I hate hunting with any gun that doesn't have a sling or carrying strap for hanging the gun over my shoulder. In-lines work well with the new generation of nylon slings, but traditional equipment should be supported by leather. If it's really "traditional," you may elect for a tied-on sling.

Every gun should have a sling or carrying strap so it can be hung over your shoulder.

Muzzleloading Essentials

Antelope Powder Horns

By Charles E. Carpenter II

The young buck antelope was not of trophy proportions, but he was the first big game animal I had taken with a muzzleloader. I wanted to celebrate his life and memorialize the hunt, and could think of no better way than to make his 7-inch horns into powder horns for use on future outings.

I sawed off the horns below the skull plate, then cut and peeled away any hide. I boiled them (outdoors) until the horns pulled away from their bases, then scraped the insides down to horn. After the horns dried, I cut squarely across the horns close to their bases, cut off about 1½ inches of the tips, and drilled ¼-inch diameter holes from the tips into the cavities. I again boiled the horns just until soft enough that their bases could be forced flush over plugs whittled from scrap pine. I let the horns dry to set the plugs in place, then glued on oversize pieces of walnut and whittled them to shape following the horns' contours.

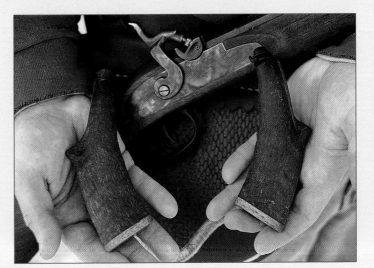

The finished powder horns.

Lastly, I whittled a stopper from one horn tip, while a woodworker friend turned another from scrap ebony. Each horn will hold a bit more than 300 grains of blackpowder, enough for three shots from my .54 caliber plains-style rifle. They will be carried in my hunting pouch along with homemade ball blocks to provide ammunition for a day's hunt.

Making muzzleloading accoutrements, such as these powder horns, is living history in the tradition of our forefathers who used simple tools and ingenuity to fashion useful accessories from the animals they harvested. Today, as then, antlers can be made into powder measures, knife handles and T-handles for short starters; leg and jaw bones can be formed into interesting and functional knife handles; hides can be turned into hunting pouches, ball bags and lock covers. Imagination and resourcefulness expand the list.

The buck wasn't quite as big as the hunters thought, but his spirit still wanders the land in the form of useful powder horns that go on every hunt.

Chapter 7

MUZZLELOADING WISDOM

S hooting in general is well-suited to tips, techniques and smoke-veiled secrets. Shooting well is a murky and mystical blend of physics, skill, knowledge, magic and luck. It's that mysterious blend with a pinch of this and a dash of that which makes any shooting work.

Muzzleloader shooting takes this concept to a higher level. Because the blackpowder shooter is so intimately involved with the process of muzzleloader shooting, success is found not in one single thing but in a multitude of smaller things.

Attention to detail is the key to reliably making smoke when the trigger is pulled. A muzzleloader shooter can't count on technology to ensure success, and he can't depend on the "store-bought" quality of self-contained ammunition mass-produced in a sterile and soulless factory in some distant land. Rather, the muzzleloader shooter must use his own skill and knowledge instead of buying the skill and knowledge of others.

The basics are easy to learn, but a mastery of the sport will take a lifetime of learning the subtle nuances that make up the whole of the sport. It's the little things that count ... and the big things too. Some of it's voodoo and some of it's skill, but it's all knowledge and it's all necessary.

A Detail Game
Every Step of the Way

From loading to shooting well to beating bad weather to cleaning a muzzleloader, this is truly a game of details. These nuggets of muzzleloading wisdom should help you on your journey.

Loading Up Right

• Start each day hunting with a freshly loaded gun. Trying to stretch one load through the season may sound great when you brag about it to your buddies, but it's embarrassing when they find out how that buck you've been after escaped. Shoot or unload the gun each night, clean it right away and put it in a warm place so that any moisture will evaporate during the night. Then reload in the morning following correct loading procedure.

• Before loading a clean gun, run a snug, dry patch down the bore to remove any oil, grease or moisture.

• Always fire several caps before loading so that any residual oil or moisture is blown out of the fire channel.

• Before loading, fire your last cap with the muzzle close to a loose, dry leaf or small crumpled piece of paper. If the object moves, you have a clear channel. If not, something is plugged.

• When using Pyrodex Pellets, make sure you place the black end toward the ignition source.

• Always use the correct powder designation for your gun. In most big game hunting rifles, that will be FFg. Using a different granulation can cause higher pressures, erratic velocities and poor accuracy. The same applies to all blackpowder substitutes. For most hunting rifles, Pyrodex RS or Select is the correct choice. Hodgdon does recommend using Pyrodex P in rifles if the charge is reduced by 10 percent. They also note that it works best in calibers of .45 or less.

• Always, always, measure Pyrodex by volume and not grain weight. In fact, muzzleloader propellants should always be loaded by volume, not by weight.

Fire your last cap before loading with the muzzle close to a loose, dry leaf or small crumpled piece of paper.

• When loading Pyrodex pellets, seat the bullet firmly on top of the pellets, but do not apply enough pressure to crush the pellet. Crushed pellets will not shoot as accurately.

• Never use anything but blackpowder or an approved substitute in any muzzleloader. The one exception may be Savage's muzzleloader designed to be used with smokeless powder.

• When loading full caliber conical bullets, be careful to align the bullet squarely with the bore when starting. Tipped bullets are inaccurate bullets.

• Be careful not to deform any bullet's soft lead nose when loading. This will hurt accuracy.

• Forcing a bullet down a severely fouled bore will deform the bullet and/or damage the sabot, causing poor accuracy.

• The best accuracy with Pyrodex Pellets is achieved with sabot bullets that are the closest to bore diameter. That is, .45 bullets work better in .50 caliber muzzleloaders than do .44 caliber bullets. In a .54 muzzleloader the best bullet is .50 caliber. Smaller bullets do not perform well at all. Both Speer and Barnes make .50 caliber bullets suitable for muzzleloader use.

• Load with the same seating pressure each time. Remember that compressed blackpowder burns more consistently than loose or uncompressed blackpowder.

• Try an over-the-powder wad such as the Wonder Patch, sold by Ox-Yoke Originals, between the powder and bullet. These pre-lubed patches cushion the bullet, protect the base from hot gases and help to cut fouling. All this can add up to better accuracy.

• Replace the nipple on your muzzleloader often and always start the hunting season with a fresh nipple. Eroded nipples can be dangerous because they allow too much gas to blow back. Also, eroded nipples can lead to misfires.

• When charging a flintlock, always have the frizzen in the "open" position and the hammer in the half-cock position. This ensures that if the hammer falls while you are loading, it can't strike the frizzen and spark, causing a premature ignition. It goes without saying that this would be dangerous to the person loading the gun or to any bystanders, and would be a very bad thing.

• Always trim off any excess leather around a new flint. An oil-soaked leather can catch fire and smolder, causing premature ignition.

• The key to accuracy is consistency. Always load each time with exactly the same procedure and same ramrod pressure. Never "bounce" a ramrod on the seated bullet. It is impossible to achieve consistency with this technique. Bouncing only deforms bullets and causes erratic seating pressures. Better to "push" solidly on the ramrod with the same pressure every time you load the gun. When loading with loose blackpowder or Pyrodex, instead apply at least 40 pounds of pressure. Learn to apply the same amount of pressure each time you load. The consistency will lead to better accuracy.

• After determining the best bullet and powder charge for your rifle, use a felt pen to mark the ramrod even with the muzzle. By putting the ramrod down the barrel, you can tell at a glance if the gun is loaded and if you have the correct charge and bullet in the gun.

• Usually, a muzzleloader will shoot to different points of impact with a clean or fouled barrel. Choose one or the other and sight in with the barrel in that condition, then hunt with it the same way.

• Always use a rod-guide to protect your muzzle crown when cleaning or loading. Damage to the crown can occur during cleaning or loading, particularly with metal ramrods. A gun with a damaged crown will never be accurate.

• Most guns, particularly when shooting bullets with sabots, will shoot more accurately if you clean the barrel each time you shoot. Instead of a complete cleaning between each shot, try a couple of passes with a patch lubricated with Wonder

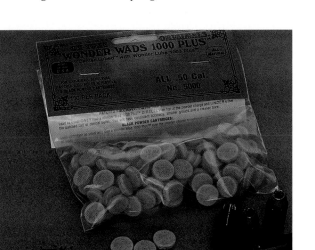

An over-the-powder wad, such as the Wonder Patch sold by Ox-Yoke Originals, can improve accuracy.

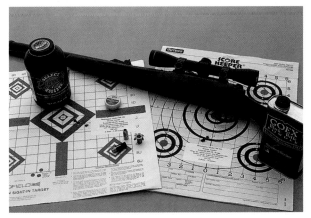

The key to muzzleloading accuracy is consistency.

Lube 1000 between shots. You can buy pre lubricated patches, or lube your own. You can follow with a dry patch, or leave the lube in the barrel. Either way, do it the same for every shot. For best results, make the same number of passes through the bore each time, both with the lubed patch and the dry patch.

• Remember that fouled barrels will corrode, so unless you are using a gun or bullet that requires a fouled barrel, such as a White Muzzleloader or Black Belt bullets, choose a clean barrel.

• When using a bullet or gun that requires a fouled bore, you can load the gun and then run a patch saturated with Wonder Lube 1000 down the bore to help protect it from corrosion. This will affect point of impact, so always load the same way when sighting in your rifle. After determining the best bullet and powder charge for your rifle, use a felt pen to mark the ramrod even with the muzzle. By putting the ramrod down the barrel, you can tell at a glance if the gun is loaded and if you have the correct charge and bullet in the gun.

• If you clean between shots, use exactly the same steps each time. If you use one wet patch followed by two dry patches, do it the same way every time. Any variation can cause the shot to be

Speed loaders are faster than digging around for separate components.

out of your group. Always pop a cap or two to clear the fire channel after cleaning and before loading again.

• After cleaning, count your patches—what went in better come out. A patch left in a gun when you are excited or tired can come back to haunt you. Believe me. I know a great 10-point Texas buck that is alive because I was in a hurry and left a patch in the gun. The sound of only the cap going off is one we both will remember for a long time.

• Use speed loaders for hunting. They are faster and less bulky to carry than separate components.

• Always wear protective glasses when firing a muzzleloader. The very nature of the ignition system allows gas to blow back through the nipple and potentially cause injurious debris to fly. How much shooting and hunting will you be doing when you are blind?

SHOOTING WELL

Shooting accurately and consistently consists of much more than just aiming and pulling the trigger.

• Don't try to make your muzzleloader a modern rifle; it can't be done. Blackpowder pressures restrict velocity, so take a tip from the hunters who used blackpowder for centuries: Increase power by using bigger, heavier bullets, not by trying to make them go faster. The ultra-light sabot bullets may have more paper energy, but they are terrible game bullets.

• Marketing people make a science of studying human behavior. It has not been lost on them that the last couple of generations of hunters have been velocity-oriented. This is fine and even desirable with modern rifles and bullets, but muzzleloaders are not modern rifles and can never perform the same way that they do.

• Do not succumb to the siren song of the marketing tempters. Ultra-high velocity (by muzzleloader standards) is not the answer for better big game performance. This is particularly true when these velocities are obtained with small diameter, lightweight bullets. Muzzleloaders are close-range firearms that depend on hunting skills to set up the shot in a reasonable range. Then muzzleloaders depend on bullet weight and diameter to kill game. Why do you think they drill those big holes in the barrel?

• No blackpowder muzzleloader is a legitimate 200-yard hunting gun. Muzzleloader hunting is about hunting skills and getting close to the game. If you want to shoot at long range, use a modern rifle, or better yet, stick with paper targets.

• Practice shooting from all field positions you may encounter while hunting.

• Use a rest to steady your gun whenever possible while hunting. In the field, rests include trees, rocks, fenceposts or your backpack, or you can bring forked sticks with you. Underwood and Stoney Point both make fold-up crossed sticks (shooting sticks) that you carry on your belt.

• Remember, your only connection to the animal you are shooting is the bullet. Don't skimp here; use the best bullet you can afford and choose it for terminal ballistics (what happens when it hits the deer) more than for accuracy. A good bullet that shoots well is better than a super-accurate bullet that performs poorly in game. There are some outstanding hunting bullets on the market today.

• Consider full caliber conical bullets. Muzzleloaders have big holes drilled in the barrel for a reason; they are designed to shoot big bullets. Full caliber bullets are excellent and often the best bullet for hunting.

• For big game such as elk or moose, but also for deer, consider heavy flat-nosed, hard-cast bullets with a sabot. They penetrate well and handgun hunters have known for years that they are deadly. You can make your own or buy them from commercial bullet casters. For .50 caliber guns I use the RCBS 45-405-FN bullet mold, using a hard alloy. I size them to .451 and use a long sabot. Accuracy is excellent and they work great on game. Similar bullets called "Harvester" are available from C&D Special Products.

• If you are using sabot bullets, make sure that the bullet's impact velocity rating is consistent with your gun's velocity capability. Many pistol bullets are not designed for the higher velocities of muzzleloaders and can fail on big game.

• Pyrodex pellets burn a little faster than Pyrodex powder. This is primarily because with the hole up the center, combined with the pellet shape, they have more exposed surface area to burn at any given time. This creates a quicker time to peak pressure and quicker energy release.

• Match your bullets to the gun's rate of twist. A slow twist, such as 1:66, requires the use of patched round balls. Sabot bullets work best with 1:28 or something similar. A twist rate of 1:48 is good for most conical bullets and will usually work with round balls. A faster twist rate will usually work better than a slower twist rate with a given bullet. For example, if your bullet calls for a 1:55 twist rate, a 1:48 will likely shoot more accurately than a 1:66 twist rate.

• Pressures can vary with different bullets. Weight is one factor, but so are diameter variations in some bullets. Also, variations on drag are

Longer barrels and larger powder charges generally provide higher velocities.

caused by materials used in sabots or in the bullets themselves.

• Muzzleloader propellants have a point of diminishing returns, where adding more powder produces a proportionally lower gain in velocity. It is pointless to increase the propellant charge weight beyond this point. It will boost recoil, reduce accuracy and give little gain in velocity or energy.

• Why do very light powder charges often result in poor accuracy? It's usually due to the bullet's failure to obturate or expand in the bore to make good contact with rifling. Also, because of the slow velocities, the bullet is not rotating fast enough to stabilize.

• Blackpowder is not a compound. It is an intimate mixture of saltpeter, charcoal and sulfur in a 75:15:10 ratio. There have been many variations of the mix over the years, as well as different manufacturing processes. Do not assume all powders are created equal. When switching brands of blackpowder or using a substitute powder, always reduce your loads and work up again to the performance level you are used to achieving from that gun.

• Properly stored blackpowder has a very long shelf life, but improperly stored muzzleloading propellants can deteriorate rapidly. Some substitute powders have a limited shelf life, particularly after they are opened. Check with the manufacturer before hunting with old powder. Better yet, use the old stuff for practice and buy a new supply for hunting each year.

• Muzzleloader powders burn from outside inward (surface burning). Kernel size is an important factor in regulating burn rate. Burning rate affects pressure, velocity and accuracy. Use only the size powder recommended for your gun.

• Why do Minni Balls not work well with large powder charges? Part of the problem is that the thin skirts will "flair" or distort from the propellant pressures still acting on them when they first leave the barrel. Also, the propellants burn hot enough to damage thin skirts. This is compounded when the hot gases are allowed into the hollow base, increasing the surface area they can heat.

• Longer barrels generally provide higher velocities with larger powder charges. This is because blackpowder and substitutes are relatively slow-burning powders. A longer barrel allows them more time to burn and act on the bullet. Short barrels are easier to use in the field. A trade-off in velocity for convenience.

• Develop loads for accuracy in 5-grain rather than 10-grain increments. You could skip the best charge weight by using 10-grain increments.

• Always sight in your muzzleloader from a solid rest, such as sandbags on a shooting bench.

• Where legal, use a scope on your muzzleloader. Scopes don't make a gun more accurate, but they do make it easier to aim. This is particularly true for hunters past 40 years of age who may not have the eyesight of their youth. Scopes are also much brighter and easier to use in the woods than iron sights.

• Periodically while hunting, and particularly after transporting a muzzleloader by car or 4-wheeler, check to make sure the bullet is still seated tight against the powder charge and has not slipped ahead. This is especially important if you are loading in a clean barrel. Powder fouling can help hold a bullet in place.

• Muzzleloaders have longer "lock time" than modern guns. It's important to follow through. That is, to maintain your sight picture until well after the gun has fired. This ensures that you stay

Muzzleloaders are close range firearms that depend on hunting skills to set up the shot in a reasonable range.

Match the bullet to the game you are hunting.

Where legal, use a scope on your muzzleloader.

on target until the bullet has left the bore. This takes practice and concentration.

BEAT BAD WEATHER

Here's how to beat bad weather when you're muzzleloading.

• On rainy days, stretch a piece of black electrical tape over the muzzle of your gun and another around the barrel near the muzzle to hold the first one in place. This will keep water out of the barrel.

• After capping the nipple, seal around the base of the cap with fingernail polish. This eliminates any possibility of water entering around the cap. Many of the products using a plastic collar around the cap can cause misfires. You can do this when the weather is good too.

• Fouling, dirt, ice or snow can slow the striker fall on an in-line muzzleloader and cause a misfire. Keep the action very clean and well-lubricated with an all-temperature lubricant. While hunting, protect the striker from the elements and never allow snow or ice to build up in the action.

• Always protect your speed loaders from moisture. Don't forget that sweat is moisture; be careful about carrying speed loaders in your pockets. Carry them in an outside pocket or in a belt pack. If it's raining, put them inside a waterproof container first. Zip-top bags work well.

Seal around the base of the cap with fingernail polish to prevent water from entering during inclement weather.

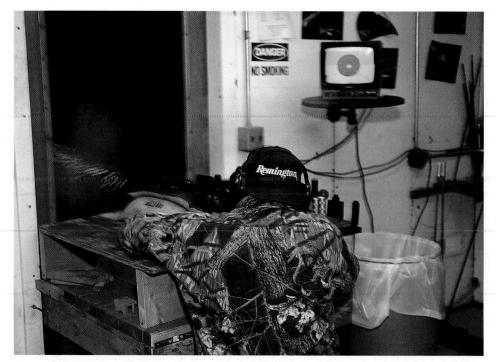

Part of sighting in a muzzleloader includes making decisions on how you're going to clean the barrel between shots ... and then doing it consistently every time.

GENERAL CLEANING TIPS & INSIGHTS

Proper cleaning is critical to accurate, effective muzzleloading. Here are some key factors.

• The white smoke from blackpowder is due primarily to its failure to convert from a solid to a gas with the efficiency of smokeless powder. Roughly half of blackpowder remains a solid after combustion, which means the bore can become caked with fouling.

• Blackpowder leaves various residues behind after burning, including: Potassium carbonate (K_2CO_3); Potassium sulfate (K_2SO_4); Potassium sulfide (K_2S); Potassium thiosulfate ($K_2S_2O_3$); Potassium thiocynate (KNCS); Carbon (C); and Sulfur (S). This is all nasty stuff to have in your precious rifle barrel. Clean your gun as soon as you are done shooting.

• Always clean your muzzleloader completely as soon as possible after shooting it. Fouling from blackpowder is hygroscopic and will attract moisture. This can cause corrosion in a very short time and quickly ruin a quality firearm.

• Never use anything with a petroleum base to clean a muzzleloading gun. The residual petroleum reacts with burning powder to create more powder fouling.

• Use Ox-Yoke's Wonder Lube 1000 Plus (also sold under other brand names) to condition your bore. Using this to clean your gun and to lube your bullets conditions the bore much like cooks condition cast-iron frying pans. The more you use it, the better the gun shoots.

• To clean small parts such as nipples or breech plugs, drop them into a small container of solvent to soak while you are working on the rest of the rifle. After soaking for a while, the powder residue will be loose and easier to clean.

• Any blackpowder gun is subject to corrosion from improper cleaning and storage. It is also subject to gas erosion from firing. Always have a gun with an unknown history inspected by a gunsmith with a bore scope. If you use your gun a lot, it's a good idea to have it checked periodically as well.

Be Safe!

Muzzleloading safety requires some extra knowledge and attention to detail.

• Don't fall for the myth that blackpowder cannot create excessive pressure. Tests have shown that blackpowder can generate 80,000 to 100,000 pounds per square inch (P.S.I.), more than enough to blow up any muzzleloader. Stick to published and tested load data. There is a reason why muzzleloaders have maximum load ratings established by manufacturers. Ignoring them can cost you your rifle, body parts or even your life.

• Blackpowder ignites easily. This is one of its most prominent features. So be safe. Keep blackpowder containers closed. Do not let a spark or flame near blackpowder. Do not apply undue pressure on blackpowder; it is percussion sensitive.

• Always put the cover back on your blackpowder container as soon as you are finished pouring out the amount you need. Never leave any powder container sitting unattended and with the top off. Any spark from smoking, shooting or even static electricity can set off an open container with catastrophic results. I have two friends who were very badly burned when a spark entered the blackpowder container they had left open.

• Not seating the bullet firmly against the propellant charge may lead to a bulge in the barrel or even a cracked barrel. It also can cost you a body part or your eyesight. So mark your ramrod for your selected load and make absolutely sure you have everything seated correctly each and every time you load your gun.

• Always hold the muzzle of a muzzleloader away from your face and body as you are loading it. If premature ignition occurs, this helps prevent injury or death.

• If you decide not to fire a flintlock after cocking the hammer, always push the frizzen forward before lowering the hammer. That way, if the hammer slips, it will not strike the frizzen and cause an unintended discharge. After lowering the hammer, bring it back to half-cock and close the frizzen.

• Never fire a muzzleloader of any kind without eye protection. Muzzleloaders are not closed-breech systems like modern cartridge guns, and there is generally debris and burning powder flying about as the gun discharges. Protect your eyesight; it's tough to hunt without it.

• If you have long hair or a beard, be very careful when firing a flintlock (or any muzzleloader, for that matter) as the fire flying from the priming pan can ignite hair and cause serious injury.

Always wear protective glasses when firing a muzzleloader.

Chapter 8

SHOOTING THE MODERN MUZZLELOADER

Most of us don't understand how the space shuttle works, but then we really don't need to. You can bet, though, that if I were flying the thing, I would learn all I could about how it operates.

It's the same with muzzleloaders. If you are going to hunt with one, it's a good idea to have at least a basic understanding of what to expect and a rudimentary knowledge of how to "drive" it.

You probably don't need to know the technical specifics of obturation, cut rifling or propellant burn profiles. You may not need to study the science of ballistics or understand the technical details of yaw, precession or rotational drift. None of this is really necessary for shooting that big 10-point buck you have been scouting all summer.

However, you should understand what to expect from your muzzleloader and have a good idea of how to achieve those expectations. You need to know the gun's strengths and weaknesses. You must understand the limitations of muzzleloader rifles and why those limitations exist.

A competent hunter knows his muzzleloader intimately and plans his hunting strategies around its performance capabilities. Knowledge is power, and power leads to success. This chapter unlocks a few of those secrets and as we all know, secrets are best when they are shared.

Now, if you will tell me exactly where that 10-point is hanging out, I'll be happy to share with you all I know about flying the space shuttle.

THE TRUTH ABOUT TODAY'S MUZZLELOADERS

*T*here is no question there are some pretty outrageous marketing claims about modern muzzleloader performance. Some marketers would have you believe their gun is somehow a mystical muzzleloader capable of slaying large dragons at 10-league distances. The hype of modern advertising makes most of us pretty skeptical, but still we wonder just how these superguns differ from "traditional" muzzleloaders and whether they are really any better in performance.

Several manufacturers are currently advertising their guns as being designed for use with three pellets or 150 grains of Pyrodex Powder. (Chris Hodgdon cautions that his company doesn't recommend more than 100-grain charges in any rifle.) One advertisement claims the same muzzle energy as a 7mm Remington Magnum, and several advertisements claim that their guns shoot flat enough to use out to 200 yards or even farther.

So what's the truth?

BETTER RIFLES

Well, there is little question that new top-shelf guns today will shoot more accurately than some traditional muzzleloaders. Rather than being inherent to the design, it is primarily a function of quality and elimination of the variables. Many of the guns are using high-quality barrels comparable to the best factory centerfire rifles, which is a big factor in accuracy.

There are other factors too. By using Pyrodex pellets and all-copper or jacketed bullets with sabots, problems with loading technique and consistency have been minimized. New, hotter ignition systems control even more variables, and the shorter lock times of the in-line guns help a little. Also, most in-lines lend themselves easily to scope mounting. While a

If you attempt to shoot at game at long range, a small miscalculation in distance can result in a wounding loss as shown by the "broken leg" on this deer target.

scope will not make any gun more accurate, it makes it easier to aim, which allows us to make more efficient use of the gun's inherent accuracy.

So yes, the guns and our ability to shoot them have led to better accuracy. While I have fired three-shot groups as small as 0.6 of an inch at 100 yards with an in-line, that is the exception rather than the rule. Some manufacturers are claiming minute-of-angle (MOA) accuracy from their guns, which is as dubious as some of the energy claims (for a definition of MOA, see the sidebar on page 135). The expected accuracy for most shooters would likely be approaching about twice MOA accuracy, which still isn't bad. Two decades ago,

The idea of using a muzzleloader is to add challenge and get closer to the game.

MOA was the accepted accuracy for most center-fire rifles, and claims to achieve 2-inch groups consistently with a muzzleloader would have been met with ridicule.

LONG-RANGE FALLACIES

As for those long shots, it is still a muzzleloader that uses either blackpowder or a substitute that mimics the performance of blackpowder. You cannot make it perform like a modern centerfire rifle.

Using a Thompson/Center Encore with three Pyrodex pellets and a Barnes 250-grain bullet, velocities were 2,107 fps (see chart on page 138), about the same as a .35 Rem. That is hardly a long-range cartridge. When sighted dead-on at 100 yards, the Encore hits 10.53 inches low at 200 yards. However, if we look at it from a point-blank range perspective, that is, to sight it so that it is never more than 3 inches above or below the point of aim, we find that with a 162-yard zero, it has a maximum point blank range (MPBR) of 189 yards. The bullet starts out with 2,465 foot-pounds of energy. At 100 yards, it retains 1,631 foot-pounds and at 200 yards, it has 1,062 foot-pounds. One thousand foot-pounds is the long-accepted minimum for deer-sized game.

With the popular Knight Disk rifle, the same 3-pellet load produced 1,971 fps, so that the MPBR for this gun is 178 yards. That is also about the point where the energy drops below 1,000 foot-pounds. At 200 yards, it is 6.53 inches low.

This all assumes that the rifle and shooter are one-hole accurate for all the distances. Considering a two-MOA accuracy, the bullet could be up to 4 inches off at 200 yards. Combined with a 6.53-inch drop, that is potentially more than 10.5

inches off the point of aim—more than enough to miss or only wound a deer.

By comparison, most modern centerfire rifles would be sighted to impact at 200 yards and will usually shoot under MOA, so the point of impact is not more than 2 inches from point of aim. Big difference.

The truth is that the trajectory of these muzzleloaders is close to the 200-grain round-nosed bullet from the .35 Rem. and is only slightly flatter than a factory 300-grain .45-70 Gov. load. Nobody has ever touted those two as long-range deer guns.

Can these in-lines kill deer at 200 yards or more? Sure. But that doesn't make them long-range deer guns for most hunters. In-lines have extended the range from our old muzzleloading rifles, but not as much as some claims would have you believe. Using these figures, they are acceptable to nearly 200 yards under perfect conditions, but who hunts under perfect conditions? Beyond that, the bullets are dropping so fast that it is all a guessing game and few hunters are good enough judges of distance, wind and all the other variables to be certain of a killing shot every time. The guns are still muzzleloaders, made for shooting close-range targets.

Forget the advertising hype. It's not about long range; it's about hunting skill and getting close. If you limit your shots to the distance you can hit a 6-inch bullseye every time, under all weather conditions and from all shooting positions, you will be a lot more successful.

If that turns out to be more than 200 yards, remind me never to shoot against you for money.

Minute-of-Angle

The accuracy of muzzleloader groups on a target are often expressed in minute-of-angle, or MOA, but what does that mean?

There are 360 degrees of angle in a full circle and 60 minutes-of-angle in each degree. One minute-of-angle equals 1.047 inches per 100 yards. So for practical purposes, 1 inch at 100 yards, 2 inches at 200 yards, 3 inches at 300 yards and so on equals one minute-of-angle.

Groups are usually measured center-to-center of the widest shots. If the distance is less than a minute of angle, or about 1 inch per each 100 yards, then the gun is said to have "minute-of-angle accuracy."

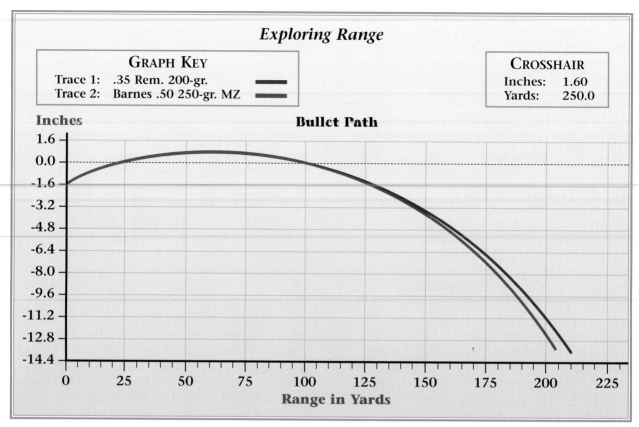

Exploring Range

GRAPH KEY
Trace 1: .35 Rem. 200-gr. —
Trace 2: Barnes .50 250-gr. MZ —

CROSSHAIR
Inches: 1.60
Yards: 250.0

We must keep the realities of muzzleloaders in perspective. For all the talk about "long-range" shooting, a .50 caliber muzzleloader loaded with three Pyrodex pellets and a 250-grain sabot bullet has a trajectory that is about the same as a .35 Remington.

Why Do Muzzleloaders Kick so Much?

Have you ever wondered why muzzleloaders seem to kick so much? Sure, it's partly because they use big, heavy bullets. But even when compared against modern rifles shooting the same-weight bullets at the same velocity, the blackpowder guns seem to kick a lot more.

It's because blackpowder is so inefficient. It takes a much heavier charge of blackpowder than it does of smokeless powder to reach the same velocity, and the weight of the powder charge is factored into the recoil.

For example, let's compare a .50 caliber muzzleloader shooting a 250-grain sabot bullet at 1,800 fps and the same bullet at the same velocity from a .44 Mag. rifle. For comparison, we will consider that both rifles weigh 7 pounds. Using a computer program to do the calculations, we find that the muzzleloader will have 39.2 foot-pounds of recoil with a recoil velocity of 19.0 fps. The .44 Mag. has 13.7 foot-pounds of recoil with a recoil velocity of 11.2 fps. In the "Apparent Felt Recoil" box, the program lists the .44 Mag. as "Moderate," but the muzzleloader is listed as "Ouch—Severe."

Why the big difference? The muzzleloader uses 120 grains of powder to achieve this velocity, while the .44 Mag. uses 25 grains of smokeless powder to achieve the same velocity.

Muzzleloaders kick more than a modern gun driving the same bullet at the same velocity. The cause: all the extra powder.

ACCURACY & REALITY

A young spokesperson from one of the major muzzleloader companies recently told me that all their guns are averaging 1.5-inch groups at 200 yards.

Now I am not about to call anybody a liar without proof, but I need to see that one with my own eyes. Group averages like that are good performance from any top-of-the-line centerfire rifle. Heck, that's good performance for a lot of varmint rifles. An average like that is something you will likely see in centerfire hunting rifles from custom makers. To find it in an off-the-shelf rifle of any kind, much less a muzzleloader, is all but unheard of. For years, I have often heard and read about muzzleloader rifles that will shoot to half a minute of angle with regularity, but never have I seen, much less shot, one. To be honest, I have serious doubts that they even exist.

WHAT IS REALITY?

Why the truth-stretching hype? In this case, the rifles in question are among the best on the market, and some of the most accurate. I have used several over the years and they all shot very well, but none of them has been capable of three-quarter minute-of-angle groups at 200 yards. So why damage a good reputation with claims that any experienced shooter will spot immediately as fraudulent?

Factory muzzleloader big game hunting rifles that will, across the board, average 1.5-inch groups at 200 yards rank with Bigfoot and green spacemen. I'd have to see it with my own eyes to believe it and even then I would suspect trickery and illusion. They simply are not part of this reality.

So what can you expect from your muzzleloader? With well-tuned loads, exact shooting and loading techniques, and a dose of luck, some in-line or bolt-action muzzleloaders can shoot three-shot groups that are sub-MOA. A very few might even be able to do it with enough regularity to claim a sub-MOA average.

However, if your in-line or bolt-action muzzleloader shoots three consecutive shots into 1.5 inches at 100 yards every time you shoot

Most of the best muzzleloader rifles will shoot groups of about two inches at 100 yards, which is outstanding accuracy.

(assuming reasonable weather conditions), you have an outstanding gun and you know how to use it correctly.

Most of the best rifles in this class will shoot at about 2 inches, which is still outstanding. A generation ago, that was considered good

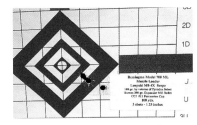

With well-tuned loads, exact shooting and loading techniques and a dose of luck, some in-line or bolt-action muzzleloaders can shoot three-shot groups that are sub-MOA.

With big critters like elk does it really matter if your gun will shoot groups that are one inch instead of two inches?

accuracy from a factory centerfire rifle and factory-loaded ammo.

Sidelocks and flintlocks should be granted a little leeway in accuracy. The locktimes are slower, the massive hammers with long falls cause a little more disturbance, and if you are shooting conical bullets or round balls, which I suspect see more use in this style rifle, they are more sensitive about loading technique. If your sidelock rifle shoots regularly into a 3-inch group at 100 yards, I would call it a keeper.

These standards are for the better guns on the market. For the lower-priced guns that may not have the same tolerance levels for fit and finish, you must make some allowances. Give them at least 1 inch more at 100 yards.

Remember, a muzzleloader is a close-range hunting gun. A moose with 1.5 feet of kill zone will not care if your gun is capable of shooting into 1 or 2 inches at 50 yards.

You don't want a gun that scatters its shots like buckshot from a broken shotgun, but don't get hung up on expecting benchrest accuracy either. Most of us just get too hung up on hair-splitting accuracy.

TESTING FOR THE TRUTH

I tested three in-line muzzleloaders with several bullets, to illustrate how some guns prefer one bullet to another. While this is representative of the accuracy potential for most muzzleloaders, it should not be taken as an absolute indication of the accuracy for these bullets and guns. Only one group was fired to access the potential for each load. Further testing would be needed before settling on a single load for hunting.

Procedures. Testing was done with four bullets: two sabot and two full caliber. All charges were 100 grains, by volume, of Pyrodex Select, unless noted otherwise. The Remington was also tested with some other powders. All groups were three shots at 100 yards, fired from a benchrest.

I cleaned between each shot by scrubbing the bore with a patch soaked in Rusty Duck Black Off, followed by two dry patches. I then snapped two caps on the empty gun to ensure that the ignition channel was clear.

Where necessary, the bullets were started with a starting tool and then seated with the supplied rod using the Barnes Muzzleload Bullet Alignment

The only way to test the true accuracy of a muzzleloader is from a bench rest.

col was maintained and the next shot was in the group. The flyer was ignored and the three correctly loaded shots were measured. But this can serve as an illustration of the importance of consistency in any procedure used in loading and shooting muzzleloading rifles.

As testing progressed, I noticed that the tapered design of the Great Plains bullet was a big asset to loading consistency. By starting it carefully by hand, followed by more careful use of a bullet-starting tool, accuracy was greatly improved. The poor group in the Remington was not a fair indication of how well this bullet will shoot. Two shots were in less than 2 inches when the third opened the group. Because there was nothing to explain this flyer, unlike the same bullet in the Knight, the group was recorded as fired. This bullet shows promise in the Remington and more extensive testing is called for before ruling it out.

Tool to ensure correct alignment with the bore. The exception to this was the CVA, which had a tight bore and would not allow the tool to enter, so seating was done with a convex .50 jag.

This tightness seemed to be restricted to the last 2 or 3 inches of the barrel, and both bullets and patches would slide much easier after passing by that section. The tight fit did make loading the Black Belt bullets very difficult and may account for the fact they had the poorest accuracy in this rifle.

The ramrod was not "bounced" or tapped. Instead, the powder was compressed with hard, constant pressure, and all charges were compressed with an equal amount of pressure.

Testing. Consistency was the key with this or any other muzzleloader accuracy test.

When testing the Knight rifle, the cleaning protocol was varied for one shot. Loading was interrupted and I couldn't remember if I had dumped in a powder charge. The rule of thumb here is to assume that you did, so I dumped it out on the ground. I then popped a cap to burn any residual powder and cleaned the barrel again. In effect, this meant that the barrel was cleaned twice. The result was a flyer that was 5 inches right of group center. After that shot, the cleaning proto-

The Black Belt Bullet is sized to land diameter and is held in alignment with the bore by the plastic cup at the base. It is easy to load and doesn't suffer from the "maiming" that often occurs when loading tight-fitted groove diameter bullets. The bullet is designed to upset upon firing and fill the grooves. As noted, the tight bore of the CVA gun made this very difficult to load, but was the exception, as the bullet has been tested in a variety of guns with no other notable problems.

Certainly experimenting with different charge weights or powders will improve group size with some bullets in any of the rifles. For example, in the Remington group sizes were improved considerably by using blackpowder instead of Pyrodex. However, this test was designed to remain constant throughout, so a "standard" charge of 100 grains of Pyrodex was settled on for all bullets and guns.

RESULTS

Remington. The rifle showed a definite preference for sabot bullets in general and the Barnes Expander-MZ solid-copper bullets in particular. The best 3-shot group was a 100-yard group that measured only .6 inch using this bullet and FFg blackpowder. As noted on the chart, this bullet performed best in this test as well, with a 1.25-inch group.

The Hornady XTP 300-grain .44 bullet with a sabot shot very well in the Remington, with a group of 2.1 inches. This is a good bullet for those who insist on using pistol bullets.

In showing the Remington's preference for sabot-style bullets, neither of the full caliber bullets tested shot quite as well as those with a plastic sabot. The overall average group size was 3.88 inches and the top three averaged 2.35 inches. However, the Remington did have the best single group of all rifles tested.

Knight. This rifle was the best performer overall in accuracy and really didn't shoot anything poorly. Group sizes averaged 2.66 inches. If we take the best three groups, the average shrinks to 1.9 inches.

The Knight rifle is extremely well made and is light and trim so that it carries well in the field. The stock had a little too much drop and needs a higher comb for comfortable shooting with a scope. The primary criticism comes in the price. It is very expensive compared to the other rifles tested. While the Knight's accuracy on average was better than the Remington's, the Remington shot tighter "best" groups.

You can expect excellent performance like this from all Knight rifles.

CVA. When you play with the "big boys," you are in tough company. It is surprising that a rifle at this price can perform as well as this one did. It actually came in second, topping the Remington in overall accuracy with an average group of 3.12 inches. But remember that the Remington's average improves to 2.35 inches if the poor group with the Hornady Great Plains bullet is discounted. If we also discount the largest group for the CVA, we find that it has 2.66-inch average, making its difference from the Remington all but insignificant. It also had the highest average velocity.

The rifle preferred the sabot bullets, but shot the Hornady Great Plains full caliber very well. With the safety features and price of this gun, it has to be recommended as an excellent buy.

Remington Model 700 ML

Bullet	Powder & Charge	Velocity	100-Yard Group Size in Inches
Barnes 300-grain Expander-MZ Sabot	Pyrodex Select 100-grain	1,520 fps	1.25
Barnes 300-grain Expander-MZ Sabot	GOEX FFg 100-grain	1,479 fps	0.6*
Hornady .44 300-grain XTP Sabot	Pyrodex Select 100-grain	1,514 fps	2.1
Cast 405-grain Sabot	Pyrodex Select 100-grain	1,370 fps	2.0*
Black Belt Bullets 348-grain	Pyrodex Select 100-grain	1,363 fps	3.7
Hornady .50 Great Plains 385-grain	Pyrodex Select 100-grain	1,390 fps	8.5
Barnes 300-grain Expander-MZ Sabot	Black Mag 2 Blackpowder Substitute 100-grain	1,229 fps	5.8*
Barnes 300-grain Expander-MZ Sabot	Black Canyon Blackpowder substitute120-grain	1,156 fps	3.8*

Accuracy with Various Bullets

Knight Magnum Elite

Bullet	Powder & Charge	Velocity	100-Yard Group Size in Inches
Barnes 300-grain Expander-MZ Sabot	Pyrodex Select 100-grain	1,501 fps	2.3
Hornady .44 300-grain XTP Sabot	Pyrodex Select 100-grain	1,572 fps	2.3
Black Belt Bullets 405-grain	Pyrodex Select 100-grain	1,437 fps	1.8
Hornady .50 Great Plains. 410-grain	Pyrodex Select 100-grain	1,335 fps	1.6

CVA Apollo Eclipse

Bullet	Powder & Charge	Velocity	100-Yard Group Size in Inches
Barnes 300-grain Expander-MZ Sabot	Pyrodex Select 100-grain	1,579 fps	2.4
Hornady .44 300-grain XTP Sabot	Pyrodex Select 100-grain	1,546 fps	1.9
Black Belt Bullets 405- grain	Pyrodex Select 100-grain	1,394 fps	4.7
Hornady .50 Great Plains 410-grain	Pyrodex Select 100-grain	1,402 fps	3.5

Notes: All powder charges by volume. Groups were three shots at 100 yards, measured center to center. Percussion caps were CCI #11. The Knight rifle used CCI Large Rifle Magnum Primers. Velocities were measured 10 feet from muzzle with an Oehler 35P Chronograph.

* Not included as part of the actual test. This data is included for comparison only.

BALLISTICS & RANGE

*L*aser rangefinders have made measuring distance to the target easy, and anybody can read a drop chart and figure out where to hold on a long shot. But from what distance is it ethical to shoot? That varies with every shooter. However, I have determined some guidelines that will help you find the maximum distance that you should be shooting at game.

You can only find this maximum range by shooting your gun under a variety of conditions and from several hunting positions. It might take several shooting sessions to figure it all out, but you should be practicing regularly anyway. And this idea gives you a goal to work toward while practicing. Once you determine your maximum shooting zone, stick with it rigidly in the field.

The first criteria for how far it's ethical to shoot at game is the maximum distance that you can hit a six-inch circle with every shot from hunting positions and under hunting conditions.

TWO CRITERIA

The first criterion for finding your maximum range is defined by the maximum distance that you can hit a 6-inch circle with every shot from different hunting positions and under different hunting conditions. This means in a moderate wind, while it is raining or snowing or under marginal light.

The second criterion for deer and antelope is that the bullet at your maximum distance must still carry at least 1,000 foot-pounds of energy. If it does not, you should not shoot past the distance where the bullet's energy drops below that level. Also, for deer, the bullet should weigh at least five times its muzzle diameter. That is, 225 grains for a .45 caliber, 250 grains for a .50 caliber and 270 grains for a .54 caliber muzzleloader.

For deer and antelope, the bullet should retain at least 1,000 foot-pounds of energy at the distance you are shooting.

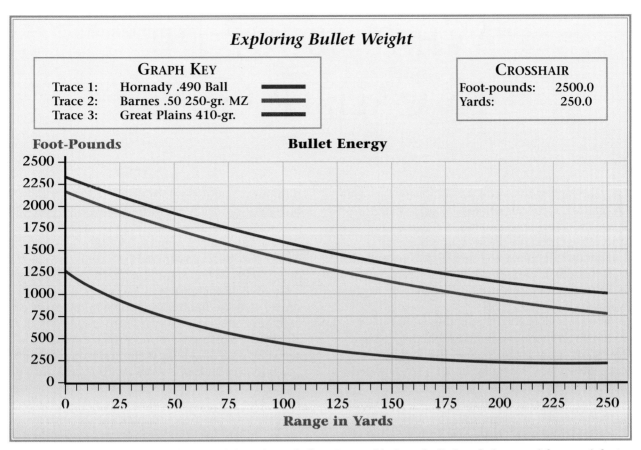

Exploring Bullet Weight

GRAPH KEY

Trace 1:	Hornady .490 Ball
Trace 2:	Barnes .50 250-gr. MZ
Trace 3:	Great Plains 410-gr.

CROSSHAIR

| Foot-pounds: | 2500.0 |
| Yards: | 250.0 |

Foot-Pounds   **Bullet Energy**

Range in Yards

Muzzleloaders are designed to work best with large, heavy bullets. Because blackpowder limits velocity potential, energy is best increased by increasing bullet weight. Heavier bullets also retain energy better downrange than light bullets.

MAINTAINING ENERGY

To maintain 1,000 foot-pounds of energy, a 225-grain bullet must have about 1,400 fps of velocity remaining when it hits the critter. For a 250-grain bullet to maintain 1,000 foot-pounds, it must retain about 1,350 fps. For a 270-grain bullet to generate 1,000 foot-pounds of energy, it will need about 1,290 fps of remaining velocity. Most manufacturers will supply load and ballistics data for their bullets that can help you determine where this distance occurs with your gun.

These numbers are for deer and antelope. I wouldn't change the shooting requirements for moose and elk because if anything, they require even more careful shot placement. But I would increase the minimum bullet weight requirements to six times the diameter and increase the retained energy requirement to 1,500 foot-pounds.

Bears need even more precise shot placement and have smaller kill zones. Keep the ballistics criteria for moose and elk, but cut the shooting distance by at least 25 percent. Cutting it in half is even better.

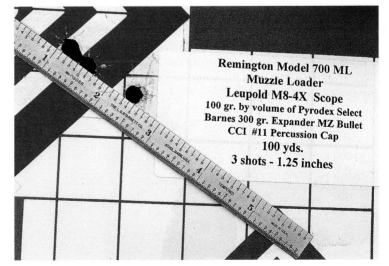

Remington Model 700 ML
Muzzle Loader
Leupold M8-4X Scope
100 gr. by volume of Pyrodex Select
Barnes 300 gr. Expander MZ Bullet
CCI #11 Percussion Cap
100 yds.
3 shots - 1.25 inches

How well you shoot your rifle is a big part of the equation on how far it's ethical to shoot at game.

WHAT ABOUT THE .45 CALIBER GUNS?

The reported velocity figures for the new generation of .45 caliber muzzleloaders designed for 150-grain powder charges are certainly impressive. Even if velocity claims are a bit inflated by the marketing people, it is inarguable that this rifle is exploring new territory in terms of bullet speed. But how does it all shake out in the real world?

The .45 caliber Knight rifle fires a .40 caliber, solid-copper, hollow-point, sabot bullet. Using a 150-grain equivalent charge of five Pyrodex 30-grain pellets, the 150-grain bullet has a reported muzzle velocity of 2,640 fps.

When sighted dead-on at 100 yards, it strikes 7.29 inches low at 200 yards. If we look at it from a point-blank-range perspective with a 6-inch kill zone—that is, to sight it so that it is never more than 3 inches above or below the point of aim—we find that with a 186-yard zero, it has an maximum point blank range (MPBR) of 214 yards. The bullet starts out with 2,322 foot-pounds of energy, at 100 yards it retains 1,362 foot-pounds and at 200 yards it has 754 foot-pounds. Remember that most experts agree that 1,000 foot-pounds is the minimum energy level for deer-sized game; the bullet crosses below that threshold at just past 150 yards.

By comparison, Federal's .270 Win. 150-Grain Nosler Partition factory load has a muzzle velocity of 2,850 fps. When sighted dead-on at 100 yards, it strikes 3.45 inches low at 200 yards, about half the drop of the muzzleloader. The MPBR using a 6-inch kill zone has a 240-yard zero and an MPBR of 282 yards, which is 68 yards farther than the muzzleloader. The .270 Win. bullet starts out with 2,706 foot-pounds of energy. At 100 yards, it retains 2,344 foot-pounds and at 200 yards, it has 2,021 foot-pounds. This is well more than twice the 200-yard retained energy of the .45 muzzleloader bullet. The .270 Win. doesn't drop below 1,000 foot-pounds of energy until past 600 yards.

BIG DIFFERENCE

Although both guns are firing the same weight bullets, the .270 starts out about 200 fps faster, but that hardly accounts for the big differences downrange. Even if we could increase the muzzleloader's velocity to equal the .270 Win.'s, at 100 yards the muzzleloader bullet will be moving 449 fps slower than the .270 Win., a 17 percent difference. At 200 yards, the velocity difference is 811 fps, which is 33 percent slower. In other words, even though they started out equal, the muzzleloader is able to retain only two-thirds as much velocity as the .270 Win. by the time they reach the 200-yard mark.

With a 100-yard zero and equal muzzle velocity, the muzzleloader will impact almost 2.5 inches lower than the .270 Win. at 200 yards. At 250 yards, it drops 6.02 inches more than the .270 Win., very nearly doubling the amount of drop of the .270. With a 6-inch kill zone, the MPBR of the muzzleloader is 228 yards, which is 54 yards less than the .270 Win.

The energy levels are identical at the muzzle, but at 100 yards the muzzleloader has 727 foot-pounds less energy than the .270 Win. This is

Muzzleloaders depend on bullet diameter for killing power. With all else equal, big bullets are always more lethal than small bullets.

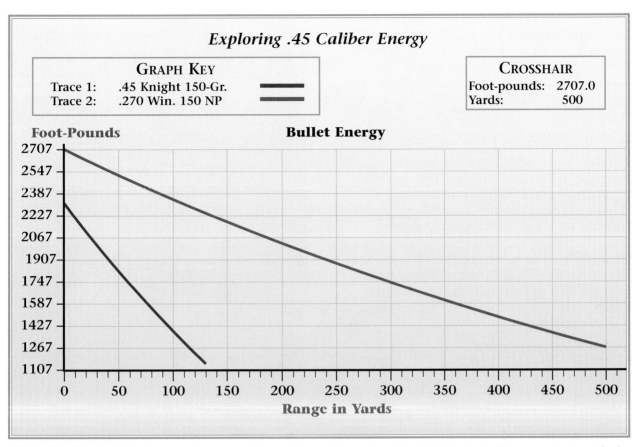

Exploring .45 Caliber Energy

GRAPH KEY
Trace 1: .45 Knight 150-Gr.
Trace 2: .270 Win. 150 NP

CROSSHAIR
Foot-pounds: 2707.0
Yards: 500

Bullet Energy

Foot-Pounds

2707
2547
2387
2227
2067
1907
1747
1587
1427
1267
1107

0 50 100 150 200 250 300 350 400 450 500

Range in Yards

While .45 caliber muzzleloaders are often compared to modern cartridges such as the .270 Winchester, this comparison is misleading. The sleeker modern bullets retain energy much better at long range than muzzleloader bullets, which rapidly shed their energy.

31 percent less. At 200 yards, the muzzleloader has 1,112 foot-pounds less energy. At this range, the muzzleloader has 55 percent less energy than the .270 Win.

INVESTIGATING BALLISTICS & PENETRATION

Obviously, the difference between the two grows larger as the distance increases. The reason is simple: ballistic coefficient (BC).

BC is a number that indicates the "aerodynamics" of a bullet. It measures how well a bullet is able to "slice" through the air and retain its velocity. The .270 150-grain Nosler Partition bullet has a BC of .465 while the 150-grain Knight muzzleloader bullet has a BC of .135. There are many factors affecting BC, including bullet shape, but the difference between the Nosler bullet and the Knight muzzleloader bullet is primarily because of the fact that while the bullets weigh the same, the muzzleloader bullet is .40 caliber, so it packs its weight into a shorter, larger bullet.

Then there is the question of penetration. The muzzleloader bullet is larger and so displaces more tissue. Assuming that both bullets expand to twice their original size, the muzzleloader will always displace more tissue than the .270 bullet as it penetrates. That means that to penetrate equal distances, the muzzleloader bullet will require more energy than the .270 bullet. But remember that at every distance beyond the muzzle, the muzzleloader has less energy. Also remember that the energy gap grows larger as the range increases.

Sectional density. The usual measure of a bullet's penetration potential is the sectional density (SD). Sectional density is a number that considers the bullet weight relative to its diameter. The heavier the bullet within a diameter, the higher the sectional density.

With all else equal, the higher the SD, the better the bullet will penetrate. The 150-grain .270 bullet has an SD of .279 while the 150-grain .40 caliber muzzleloader bullet only has a sectional density of .134, which is less than half. So, theoretically speaking, with all else equal, the muzzleloader bullet will penetrate less than half as well as the .270's bullet.

In order for its SD to equal the .270's, the muzzleloader bullet would have to weigh 312 grains. Of course, then it would be impossible to achieve the velocities that the lighter bullet reaches.

CONCLUSIONS

It's all "Voodoo Ballistics!" Blackpowder muzzleloaders are not modern rifles and they can never achieve the ballistic performance that a modern, smokeless-powder, metallic-case rifle can reach. There is always a trade-off. Poor energy levels, steep trajectories and poor penetration are a recipe for only wounding game. Muzzleloaders are close-range guns designed to fire large, heavy bullets at relatively slow velocities. That's not going to change no matter how much the marketing people cook the numbers.

Why risk a trophy of a lifetime with something as foolish as using a marginal caliber or bullet?

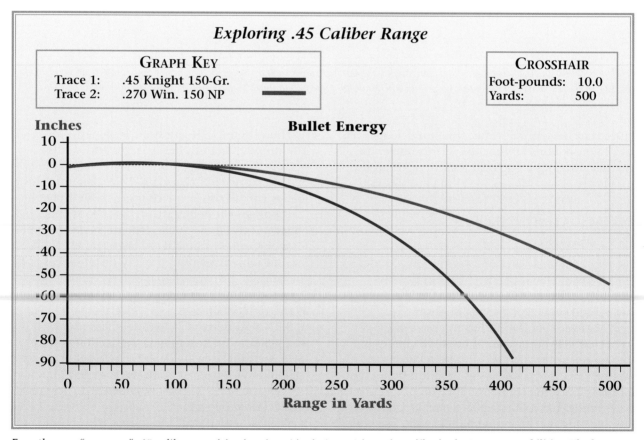

Even the new "magnum" .45 caliber muzzleloaders do not begin to match modern rifles in downrange capabilities. The lower ballistic coefficient of the muzzleloader bullet will cause its trajectory to drop much more quickly.

DEALING WITH RAIN & WET

The Vermont muzzleloader deer season was ready to go down in history as the wettest on record. I think it rained every day, but never in the nine-day season did the sky dump more water than it did on the final day.

By that time of the year, the deer have been hunted for more than two months and most are hiding in the thick stuff, trying to keep their hides bullet-hole free.

Because it's also the only time we can shoot does with firearms, we try to do some management hunting as well as giving the kids (and adults) a chance to fill their doe permits. We have a tradition of gathering a bunch of hunters at the Mason Farm in southwest Vermont to try and drive the uncooperative deer.

Just before dark on the last day, ten or so of us gathered at the edge of the woods—soggy, discouraged and almost glad it was over for another year. Picking an old abandoned car that had been parked at the edge of the field since before any of us were born, we one by one shot at a spot on the door to unload our guns.

After the first three muzzleloaders misfired, I stepped up and bragged I would show them how it's done. "Attention to detail," I explained, "is the key to muzzleloader reliability." I bragged that my muzzleloaders always go off. I aimed at the old car and pulled the trigger. The cap fired, but that's all. Amid the jeers and taunts, each of the other hunters took their turn. Only one gun went off on the first try.

That hunter had shot at a couple of deer during the day, one of them only a few moments earlier, so the gun had a fresh charge. (Obviously, he was not the best shot in the group!) Most of the rest of the muzzleloaders had been loaded that morning. A couple had been fired early in the day and a few

Muzzleloaders are susceptible to problems from rain and snow. Take the time to attend to detail and prevent misfires and no-fires.

had been carried hunting for several days with the same load.

But none of that mattered; all but one of the rifles failed to fire on the first attempt. They eventually went off, some on the second cap, but a few took several caps before firing, reminding us once again that water and blackpowder (and Pyrodex) do not play well together.

Obviously, in a complete deluge, it's tough to keep anything dry, and the very fact that we were out hunting in such conditions should speak volumes about the dedication of this bunch of hunters.

DON'T GET LAZY

No doubt some of the guns being subjected to that extreme weather would have problems, but it should not have been all of them.

Part of the problem was that the season had worn us all down. We should not have been experiencing rain that time of year. Usually, we expect deep snow, extreme cold and winter conditions by the time muzzleloader season rolls around. But that fall was different. It was t-shirt warm through most of October, November and early December.

Added to the almost daily rain, this fluky weather had the deer hiding in the shady side of the thick brush patches. It was one of the toughest deer seasons any of us could remember. Both the weather and the lack of success had us all worn out mentally and physically.

What I am trying to say is, we got lazy. Early in the season, with enthusiasm running high, it's easy to stay pumped up for the hunt. With a positive mental attitude comes better attention to the little things. When things are going right, we are apt to tend more enthusiastically to the details that make muzzleloader hunting successful.

By the time that last day rolled around, we were all burned out, discouraged and mentally low. We got sloppy and didn't tend to the details that would have made the difference. We neglected to weatherproof our guns and it was only the continuation of the horrible hunting season that allowed us to discover the consequences of that laziness when shooting at an "Old Buick" rather than at "Old Mossy Horns."

It's really quite simple. Blackpowder is hygroscopic: It attracts water. But if blackpowder encounters any water, it will not burn. Hunting season occurs in most places during times of transition, which usually means extreme weather. Often, "extreme weather" translates to water in some form. It might be rain, snow or even high humidity, but it's all water. To ensure that your gun will fire when the moment of truth arrives, you must keep your powder separated from that water.

Wet days like this require that a hunter "keep his powder dry."

KEEPING EVERYTHING DRY: SEAL IT UP

Make sure your gun is dry to start with and load it in a place that is protected from the rain or snow. After loading, you must seal up all the "ports of entry" where water can migrate to the powder charge.

The biggest hole in the gun is the bore. Many hunters assume that the bullet will seal the bore well enough to keep the water from reaching the powder, but that's not true. Few, if any, muzzleloader bullets form a complete seal in the bore before the gun fires. It doesn't take much space for water to creep through. The obvious solution is to keep the water from entering the barrel to begin with.

Some companies sell a muzzle mitt that will fit over the end of the barrel to seal water out. They are called by various names, but the design is instantly recognizable. You can also use the small finger cots that doctors use for some exams, which are available at drug stores. You can also use small balloons.

This "finger cot" is available in any drug store. It will help keep water from entering the muzzle of the gun.

A Simple Barrel Solution

I have found that of everything I have tried, simple, black vinyl electrician's tape works best for keeping rain out of your barrel. This tape will stretch, so when put on correctly it applies constant tension, sealing out water. No other kinds of tape work as well because they lack the elasticity of electrician's tape.

The tape should be at least 1-inch wide. Remove the ramrod and make sure the gun is wiped clean of oil and is dry. Cut a piece of tape about 8 inches long (different guns may require different lengths of tape) and hold it so it's centered over the end of the muzzle with the ends pointing to both sides of the gun. Orient the tape so that when you lay it down along the barrel, it runs parallel to the front sight without hitting it.

Now hold the tape just above the end of the bore and pull the tape until it stretches to about ¾-inch wide. Then place it over the bore. This will leave ⅛ inch on either side of a .50 caliber muzzle. Maintaining the tension, pull the tape down the

sides of the barrel and stick it without releasing the tension. Make sure to keep it stretched across the muzzle. The ends should be well past the front sight and any rod thimbles so that they end in a place where the barrel is free from obstructions.

When applied correctly, vinyl electrician's tape is excellent for keeping water out of the gun.

Now do the same with a second piece of tape, bringing it along the other side of the front sight. Try to come as close to making a cross as possible while still working around the sight and ramrod thimbles.

Finally, take at least two turns around the barrel above the ends of the tape to hold them in place. Keep tension enough to stretch the tape to three-quarters of its width. Repeat this at the next available location.

If you place the tape with care over the muzzle to ensure that the edge is at least ⅛ inch past the bore on all sides, and if you maintain tension on all the tape you place, this should seal out any water. Check the tape often during the hunt to make sure it hasn't slipped off or become damaged.

Don't worry about it affecting your shot. The tape will blow off the end of the barrel from the air being forced out the bore, long before the bullet reaches it, and it will not have a detrimental effect on accuracy. It is safe to fire the gun with tape over the bore; the tape does not have the effect that a true muzzle obstruction might.

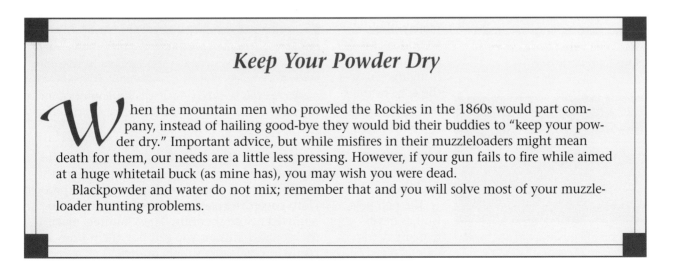

Keep Your Powder Dry

When the mountain men who prowled the Rockies in the 1860s would part company, instead of hailing good-bye they would bid their buddies to "keep your powder dry." Important advice, but while misfires in their muzzleloaders might mean death for them, our needs are a little less pressing. However, if your gun fails to fire while aimed at a huge whitetail buck (as mine has), you may wish you were dead.

Blackpowder and water do not mix; remember that and you will solve most of your muzzleloader hunting problems.

Keeping Everything Dry: Nipple & Caps

The next trouble spot is the nipple. It goes without saying that you should only use the highest quality caps that have been sealed with lacquer at the factory. The problem is that no cap is a perfect seal on the nipple, and water can migrate into the powder.

Many companies sell small plastic rings that will slide over the cap and are supposed to keep water from entering the nipple. I don't like them. I have had misfires with some guns because the rings have blocked the hammer fall. The rings also do not seal completely enough to suit me.

Instead, I carry a small bottle of fingernail polish in my kit. After placing the cap firmly on the nipple, I coat around the bottom edge of the cap and the nipple with fingernail polish. After it dries for a few minutes, I apply a second coat, bringing the edges of this coat past the edge of the first coat on both top and bottom.

The first coat should seal it completely; the second coat is for insurance. Bringing it past the edge of the first coat helps to seal any voids that may be present in the first application.

The nail polish has never had any detrimental effect

Fingernail polish can seal around a cap to prevent water from migrating into the breech.

Separate parts in the ignition system attached by screws provide potential places for water to enter.

Use a knife to remove a cap that's sealed with fingernail polish.

on the cap that I have witnessed, and I have been doing this for years. If I need to remove the cap at the end of the day, I simply use a small, sharp knife blade to scrape it off the nipple. Follow firearm safety guidelines (point the muzzle in a very safe direction) when doing this in case you encounter an accidental discharge.

Of course, you should have coated the nipple's threads well with grease before replacing it the last time you cleaned the gun. But it wouldn't hurt to use a good degreaser and clean the location where the nipple enters the gun; then seal it with nail polish. Some guns use a nipple seat that is attached with a screw; make sure that it is well sealed, as it usually will leak.

The nail polish trick works well with #11 caps, musket caps or #209 primers. The key is to simply seal up any joints. With #209 shotgun primers, you can coat the sides of the primer before you insert it into the gun.

Flintlock Challenges

Flintlocks present another problem altogether in wet weather. I think the best solution is to not use them when the weather is nasty, and fortunately, the law allows that in most places I hunt. But in Pennsylvania's woods, there is no other choice. Or maybe you wish to limit yourself to a flintlock, come hell or (literally) high water.

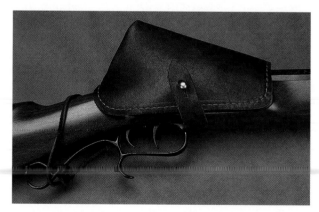

A cover like this helps keep water out of a flintlock's firing system.

Remember that not only must the powder be dry, but the frizzen must also be kept dry for the flintlock to fire. A guard of leather or waterproofed cloth covers the pan and frizzen. This must be removed before shooting. Many hunters make their own guards, or you can buy them from many muzzleloader supply outlets.

Once the pan is primed and the frizzen is closed, the joint can be sealed with grease. This helps keep the water out of the priming charge, but will easily release the frizzen when it is struck by the flint. Make sure you are using grease that is not temperature sensitive, as some grease can melt and migrate into the priming powder in hot weather or solidify in cold weather, keeping the frizzen from opening easily.

OTHER PRECAUTIONS

Your powder and caps must be stored in their original containers and kept in a cool, dry location. When dispensing powder from the can, recap it as soon as you have removed the powder you need. It is not only dangerous to keep the cap off the can, but water can enter as well.

In the field, waterproof speed loaders are the best way to carry your reloads. But even the best can leak. If I am expecting foul weather, I also put my speedloads in at least two zip-top plastic bags.

Remember too that sweat is moisture; it's easy for reloads to become contaminated simply by carrying them in your shirt pocket. It doesn't necessarily need to be hot weather, either. Any hunter who has dressed to sit in cold weather, and then dragged a buck back to the truck, knows it's possible to sweat in any temperature.

Take care when reloading on nasty days. Any water entering the bore while you are reloading may be enough to contaminate the powder charge. Always try to find some shelter when reloading. At the very least, shield the gun with your body. But be careful of water running off your hat or coat. Plan ahead so that you know where everything is and you can reload in a minimum of time. The quicker you reload, the less chance of contamination.

I try never to hunt two days with the same powder charge, no matter what the weather. While I do on occasion break this rule, usually I will fire the gun or otherwise unload it each evening at the end of the hunt.

The protocol I try to follow is to clean the bore and put the gun near a mild heat source overnight to make sure it's dry. It's best to stand it several feet away from a wood stove. Nothing beats a wood fire for drying out wet "stuff." Lacking that, place the gun near a warm air heat vent. At the very least, keep the gun in a warm, dry living area.

In the morning, reload. Practice careful loading techniques, and replace the waterproofing. The tape and nail polish only take a few minutes longer and you never know what the day will

Don't forget, snow is made from water, and blackpowder and water do not mix.

bring in terms of weather. They cause no harm in good weather and if it turns bad, they are in place before the first potentially powder-destroying raindrop falls.

On nasty days if I have a place to dry out the gun, I will shoot it midday. Then I dry it out, reload and re-waterproof. If I must remain outside, I trust in my initial waterproofing to get me through the day. Usually it does, but firing the gun and then reloading out in the wet conditions risks moisture contamination. It's a gamble, but the odds here favor the waterproofing applied when the gun is dry.

Finally, accept that water and blackpowder are like teenagers in love. No matter how extensive your attempts to keep them apart, they find a way to mate. There will be times when, no matter what you do, the gun will fail to fire.

That is both the frustration and the charm of muzzleloader hunting.

MUZZLELOADING SUPPLIERS

POWDER & BULLETS

Alliant Powder - Alliant Techsystems
Box 1 Route 114
Radford, VA 24141-0096
800-276-9337
www.AlliantPowder.com
Smokeless powder

Barnes Bullets
760 North 2600
West Lindon, UT 84042
800-574-9200
www.barnesbullets.com
MZ Expander Muzzleloader Bullets

Big Bore Express - Black Belt Bullets
7154 West State St. #200
Bosie, ID 83703
800-376-4010
www.bigbore.com
Muzzleloader bullets

Blackpowder Shooter's Resource Guide
www.sky.net/bfinch/blackpdr.htm
Online blackpowder supply source

Blount, Inc.
900 Ehlen Dr.
Anoka, MN 55303
800-627-3640
www.blount.com
Speer, CCI, RCBS, Weaver, Ram Line

Buffalo Bullet Company, Inc.
12637 Los Nietos Road, Unit A
Santa Fe Springs, CA 90670
800-423-8069
Muzzleloader bullets

C & D Special Products
309 Sequoya Drive
Hopkinsville, KY 42240
800-922-6287
www.claybusterwads.com
Harvester Hard-Cast, Flat-Nosed Sabot Muzzleloader Bullets, Sabots for muzzleloader bullets

CCI - Speer
Box 856
2299 Snake River Ave.
Lewiston, ID 83501
800-666-5761
www.cci-ammunition.com
www.speer-bullets.com
Bullets, primers, percussion caps

Century Arms International, Inc.
1161 Holland Drive
Boca Raton, FL 33487
800-527-1252
www.centuryarms.com
Shooting supplies

Clean Shot Technologies, Inc.
21218 St. Andrews Blvd.
Boca Raton, FL 33433
888-866-2532
561-477-7039
www.cleanshot.com
Black powder replacement

Combined Technology
PO Box 671
Bend, Oregon 97709
800-627-3640
Hunting bullets

Dixie Gun Works, Inc.
Box 130
Gunpowder Lane
Union City, TN 38281
901-885-0700
www.dixiegun.com
Blackpowder shooter's supplies

Federal Cartridge Co.
900 Ehlen Drive
Anoka, MN 55303-7503
800-322-2342
www.federalcartridge.com
Bullets

GOEX Black Powder
PO Box 659
Doyline, LA 71023
318-382-9300
www.goexpowder.com
Blackpowder, Clean Shot Black Powder Replica Propellant

Gonic Arms, Inc.
134 Flagg Road
Gonic, NH 03839
603-332-8456
www.gonic.com
Muzzleloaders and bullets

Gordon Wilson Jenks & Co.
104 Glenwood Drive
Westfield, MA 01085
800-835-7933
GOEX Black Powder master distributor

Hodgdon Powder Co.
Box 2932
6231 Robinson
Shawnee Mission, KS 66201
913-362-9455
www.hodgdon.com www.pyrodex.com
Pyrodex, pyrodex pellets, muzzleloader cleaning supplies

Hornady Manufacturing
PO Box 1848
3625 Old Potash Hwy.
Grand Island, NE 68803
800-338-3220
www.hornady.com
Muzzleloader bullets and accessories, blackpowder measure ammunition

Lee Precision, Inc.
4275 Hwy. U
Hartford, WI 53027
414-673-3075
www.leeprecision.com
Bullet molds

Luna Tech, Inc.
148 Moon Drive
Owens Cross Roads, AL 35763
256-725-4224
Blackpowder

Lyman Products Corp.
475 Smith St.
Middletown, CT 06457
800-225-9626
www.lymanproducts.com
Muzzleloaders and bullet molds

Midway Arms, Inc.
PO Box 718
5875 W. Van Horn Tavern Road
Columbia, MO 65203
800-243-3220
www.midwayUSA.com
**Reloading & shooting equipment
and supplies**

Mountain State Muzzleloading
Box 154-1
Rt. 2
Williamstown, WV 26187
304-375-7842
www.mtnstatemuzzleloading.com
Muzzleloading supplies

Northern Precision
329 S. James St.
Carthage, NY 13619
315-493-1711
Custom bullets

Nosler Inc.
P.O. Box 671
Bend, OR 97709
800-285-3701
www.nosler.com
Bullets

Old Western Scrounger
12924 Highway A-12
Montague, CA 96064
530-459-5445
www.ows-ammunition.com
Old ammo & shooting supplies

Ox-Yoke Originals, Inc.
34 Main St.
Milo, ME 04463
800-231-8313
www.oxyoke.com
**Pre-lubed wads and other black pow-
der shooting accessories**

Petro-Explo, Inc
7650 U.S. Highway 287
Suite 100
Arlington, TX 76001
800-588-8282
www.elephantblackpowder.com
**Elephant Black Powder & Swiss Black
Powder**

Precision Rifle
Box 12 Grp 71 RR1
Anola, MB R0E 0A0 Canada
877-828-5538
www.prbullet.com
Custom muzzleloader bullets

Ramshot Propellant
P.O. Box 158
Yellowstone Hill
Miles City, MT 59301
800-497-1007
www.ramshot.com
Smokeless Powder

RCBS
605 Oro Dam Blvd.
Oroville, CA 95965-4650
800-533-5000
www.rcbs.com
Reloading equipment

Redding Reloading Equipment
1089 Starr Road
Cortland, NY 13045
607-753-3331
www.redding-reloading.com
Reloading equipment

Sierra Bullets
1400 West Henry St.
Sedalia, MO 65301
800-223-8799
www.sierrabullets.com
Bullets

SPG Lubricant
P.O. Box 761
Livingston, MT 59047
406-222-8416
www.blackpowderspg.com
**Bullet lubricant, reloading primer for
black powder cartridges;
Publishers of Black Powder Cartridge
News**

Stoney Point Products, Inc.
PO Box 234
1822 North Minnesota St.
New Ulm, MN 56073-0234
507-354-3360
www.stoneypoint.com
**Precision shooting and reloading
equipment**

Swift Bullet Company
PO Box 27
201 Main St.
Quinter, KS 67752
785-754-3959
Bullets

Winchester Ammunition
427 N. Shamrock St.
East Alton, IL 62024-1174
800-365-2666
www.winchester.com
**Ammunition, smokeless powder and
bullets**

OPTICS

Ashley Outdoors, Inc.
2401 Ludelle St.
Fort Worth, TX 76105
888-744-4880
www.ashleyoutdoors.com
Sight systems

Burris Company, Inc.
PO Box 1747
331 East 8th St.
Greeley, CO 80632
888-228-7747
www.burrisoptics.com
Rifle scopes & sports optics

Bushnell—Sport Optics Div.
(Bausch & Lomb)
9200 Cody
Overland Park, KS 66214
800-423-3537
www.bushnell.com
Rifle scopes & sports optics

Conetrol
10225 Hwy. 123 South
Seguin, TX 78155
1-800-conetrol
www.conetrol.com
Scope mounts

Gradient Lens Corporation
207 Tremont St.
Rochester, NY 14608
800-536-0790
www.gradientlens.com
Hawkeye Precision Borescope

Kahles USA
2 Slater Rd.
Cranston, RI 02920
800-426-3089
401-734-5888
www.kahlesoptik.com
Rifle scopes

Leica Camera Inc.
156 Ludlow Ave
Northvale, NJ 07647
800-222-0118
www.leica.com
Cameras and sports optics

Leupold & Stevens, Inc.
PO Box 688
14400 NW Greenbrier Pkwy.
Beaverton, OR 97006-5790
503-526-5195
www.leupold.com
Scopes and binoculars

Millett Sights
7275 Murdy Circle
Huntington Beach, CA 92647
800-645-5388
www.millettsights.com
Sights, scopes & mounts

Nikon Inc—Sport Optics
1300 Walt Whitman Rd.
Melville, NY 11747-3064
516-547-4200
www.nikonusa.com
Sports optics

Pentax Corporation
35 Inverness Dr. E.
Englewood, CO 80112
303-799-8000
www.pentaxlightseeker.com
Sports optics

Segway Industries
Box 783
Suffern, NY 10901
914-357-5510
www.segway-industries.com
Scope leveler

Simmons/Weaver/Redfield/Orbex
201 Plantation Oak Drive
Thomasville, GA 31792
800-285-0689
www.simmonsoptics.com
Optics and mounts

Swarovski Optik
2 Slater Rd.
Cranston, RI 02920
800-426-3089
www.Kahlesoptik.com
Optics

Talley Scope Mounts
PO Box 821
Glenrock, WY 82637
307-436-8724
www.talleyrings.com
Scope mounts

Tasco
2889 Commerce Pkwy.
Miramar, FL 33025
800-368-2726
www.tascosales.com
Rifle scopes

Warne Manufacturing Co.
PO Box 38
Onalaska, WI 54650
608-781-5800
Scope mounts and rings

Williams Gun Sight Co.
PO Box 329
7389 Lapeer Rd.
Davison, MI 48423
800-530-9028
www.williamsgunsight.com
Sights

Carl Zeiss Optical, Inc.
13017 North Kingston Ave.
Chester, VA 23836
800-338-2984
www.zeiss.com
Rifle scopes & sports optics

RIFLES/WEAPONS MANUFACTURERS

Connecticut Valley Arms, Inc.
5988 Peachtree Corners East
Norcross, GA 30071
800-320-8767
www.cva.com
Muzzleloading rifles

Kahnke Gun Works
206 W. 11th St.
Redwood Falls, MN 56283
507-637-2901
www.powderandbow.com/kahnke
Muzzleloading rifles and handguns

Knight Rifles
PO Box 130
21852 Highway J46
Centerville, IA 52544-0130
515-856-2626
www.knightrifles.com
Muzzleloaders and accessories

Muzzleloading Technologies
White Muzzleloaders
25 E. Hwy. 40 (330-12)
Roosevelt, UT 84066
877-684-4867
www.shootmti.com
Blackpowder guns, bullets and accessories

Navy Arms Company
689 Bergen Blvd.
Ridgefield, NJ 07657
800-669-6289
www.navyarms.com
Reproduction guns

O.F. Mossberg & Sons, Inc.
Box 497
7 Grasso Ave.
New Haven, CT 06473
800-989-4867
www.mossberg.com
Firearms

Prairie River Arms LTD
1220 North Sixth Street
Princeton, IL 61356
800-445-1541
www.prabullpup.com
Bullpup Muzzleloader

Remington Arms Co., Inc.
PO Box 700
870 Remington Drive
Madison, NC 27025-0700
800-243-9700
www.remington.com
Firearms and ammunition

Savage Arms
100 Springdale Rd.
Westfield, MA 01085
800-370-0706
www.savagearms.com
Firearms

Sturm, Ruger & Co., Inc.
200 Ruger Rd.
Prescott, AZ 86301
800-245-5347
www.ruger-firearms.com
Firearms

Thompson/Center Arms
Box 5002
Farmington Rd.
Rochester, NH 03866
603-332-2333
www.tcarms.com
Muzzleloaders and accessories, Contender handguns and carbines

Traditions Performance Firearms
P.O. Box 776
1375 Boston Post Road
Old Saybrook, CT 06475
860-388-4656
www.traditionsmuzzle.com
Shotguns, rifles, handguns, blackpowder guns, bullets and accessories

Winchester Shooting Products
5875 West Van Horn Tavern Rd.
Columbia, MO 65203
800-243-3220
www.midwayusa.com
Rifles, shotguns & accessories

GUN CARE & CLEANING

Birchwood Casey
7900 Fuller Road
Eden Prairie, MN 55344
800-328-6156
www.birchwoodcasey.com
Gun care products

Decker Shooting Products
1729 Laguna Ave.
Schofield, WI 54476
715-359-5873
Gun vice

J. Dewey Mfg. Co., Inc.
P.O. Box 2014
Southbury, CT 06488
203-264-3064
www.deweyrods.com
High-quality gun care products, nylon-coated cleaning rods

Hoppe's—A Brunswick Company
Airport Industrial Mall
Coatesville, PA 19320
610-384-6000
www.hoppes.com
Hoppe's gun care products

Markesbery Muzzle Loaders, Inc.
7785 Foundation Drive, Suite 6
Florence, KY 41042
800-875-0121
www.markesbery.com
Rusty Duck Black Powder Cleaning Products, muzzleloader guns

Outers/Ram Line
PO Box 38
Onalaska, WI 54650
800-635-7656
www.outers-guncare.com
Outers gun care products, including Foul Out, Cleaning Rods, Ram Line Stocks

Venco Industries, Inc.
16770 Hill Top Park Pl.
Chagrin Falls, OH 44023-4500
800-232-1991
www.shooters-choice.com
Shooting and cleaning products

GENERAL SUPPLIES

Brownells, Inc.
Box 1
200 South Front St.
Montezuma, IA 50171
641-623-5401
www.brownells.com
Gunsmithing tools and equipment

Bullberry Barrel Works
2430 West Bullberry Lane
Hurricane, UT 84737
435-635-9866
www.bullbery.com
Replacement barrels

Butler Creek Corporation
290 Arden Dr.
Belgrade, MT 59714
800-423-8327
www.butler-creek.com
Shooting accessories

Cabela's
400 E Avenue A
Oshkosh NE 69190
800-237-4444
www.cabelas.com
**Guns, bullets & accessories
for muzzleloaders**

DBI Books—Book Division Krause
Publications
700 East State St.
Iola, WI 54990-0001
800-258-0929
www.krause.com
**Books on muzzleloaders, muzzle-
loader loading data books**

Green Mountain Rifle Barrel Co., Inc.
PO Box 2670
Conway, NH 03818
603-447-1095
Rifle barrels

Harris Engineering, Inc.
999 Broadway St.
Barlow, KY 42024
270-334-3633
Bipods

Knouff & Knouff, Inc.—ICC
PO Box 9912
Spokane, WA 99209
800-262-3322
www.kkair.com
Cases for firearms and bows

Michaels of Oregon Co.
PO Box 1690
Oregon City, OR 97045
503-655-7964
www.unclemikes.com
www.michaels-oregon.com
Hunting accessories

MTM Molded Products Company
PO Box 13117
Dayton, OH 45413
937-890-7461
www.mtmcase-gard.com
**Molded ammo boxes
and shooting products**

Nalpak
1937-C Friendship Dr.
El Cajon, CA 92020
888-488-3372
www.tuffpak.com
Tuffpak gun cases

National Muzzle Loading Rifle
Association
PO Box 67
Friendship, IN 47021-0067
800-745-1493
www.nmlra.org
Muzzleloading information

Oehler Research
P.O. Box 9135
Austin, TX 78766
800-531-5125
www.oehler-research.com
Ballistic chronographs

Pachmayr Ltd.
475 Smith St.
Middletown, CT 06457
800-423-9704
Handgun grips, recoil pads

Smart's Combo Muzzle Loader
49 Park St.
Northfield, NH 03276
603-286-3017
Muzzleloader's tackle box

Underwood Rifle & Pistol Rest
Box 924
Mocksville, NC 27028
336-751-9009
www.underwoodrest.com
Rifle rests

Walker's Game Ear
P.O. Box 1069
Media, PA 19063
800-424-1069
www.walkersgameear.com
**Walker's Game Ear, Walker's Sport
Glasses**

INDEX